BISHOP

William H. Willimon

BISH⊕P

The Art of
Questioning Authority
by an Authority
in Question

Foreword by Adam Hamilton

ABINGDON PRESS
NASHVILLE

BISHOP
THE ART OF QUESTIONING AUTHORITY
BY AN AUTHORITY IN QUESTION

Copyright © 2012 by Abingdon Press

This book is printed on acid-free paper.

Library of Congress Cataloging-in-Publication Data

Willimon, William H.
  Bishop : the art of questioning authority by an authority in question / William H. Willimon ; foreword by Adam Hamilton.
      p. cm.
  Includes bibliographical references (p.   ) and index.
  ISBN 978-1-4267-4229-3 (book - pbk. / trade pbk. : alk. paper) 1. Methodist Church—Bishops. 2. Christian leadership—Methodist Church. I. Title.
  BX8345.W55 2012
  262'.1276--dc23

                                                                                  2012004908

12 13 14 15 16 17 18 19 20 21—10 9 8 7 6 5 4 3 2 1

MANUFACTURED IN THE UNITED STATES OF AMERICA

To John Redmond, Jack Meadors, and all the Methodists
who got me into this

Watch over yourselves and over all the flock, of which the Holy Spirit has made you overseers, to shepherd the church of God that he obtained with the blood of his own Son.

Acts 20:28

CONTENTS

Contents

FOREWORD

It was 1987 and I had just begun my second year of seminary at Perkins School of Theology. Twenty-two years after Methodism last showed growth, few people were talking about the problems leading to its decline, and even fewer were suggesting real solutions.

One day between classes someone asked me in a whisper, "Have you read Willimon's book yet?" as though the book might be a bit too dangerous to mention aloud. I quickly bought a copy of *Rekindling the Flame* and devoured it. Dr. Willimon was then a forty-two-year-old seminary professor at Duke stating uncomfortable truths with prophetic boldness. I have that copy of *Rekindling* before me as I write this foreword. Its dog-eared pages and underlines serve as reminders of how much that book fanned the flames of my own desire to reform and renew the church.

Fast-forward twenty-four years. Willimon has spent the last two and a half decades challenging, cajoling, pushing, and prodding, most recently as the bishop of the North Alabama Conference of The United Methodist Church, seeking to lead his church to a "future with hope." Like the prophet Jeremiah, who first coined that phrase, Willimon's call for the renewal of the people of God is like a fire shut up in his bones.

The thing about prophets is that they always step on toes, irritating most of their listeners from time to time. Bishop Willimon has stepped on plenty of toes, including my own!

What makes the prophet Willimon's words easier to hear is his own self-effacing way of speaking. He takes the church and its leadership very seriously. But he doesn't take himself that seriously. His attitude is captured in the subtitle to this book, *The Art of Questioning Authority by an Authority in Question.*

Yet what leads large numbers of people to listen to him, despite the fact that they know their toes will be sore when they are done, is that he is so often right. Though occasionally I may disagree with this or that comment, I overwhelmingly find myself wanting to shout aloud, "Amen!" and "Preach!" So it is with this present volume. Reader, be warned: your toes will be stepped on, yet you likely needed this to get your feet moving. At the same time you'll also find yourself wanting to shout, "Amen!" and "Preach!"

When I finished reading this manuscript, like *Rekindling the Flame* twenty-four years ago, the pages of the manuscript were dog-eared and underlined with more than a few exclamations of "Yes!" and "I can't believe he just said that!" scattered throughout. Will has said things only a retiring bishop can say. Finishing the book, I find my commitment to the renewal of the church rekindled.

Despite its title, this book is not just for bishops. It is for every pastor and lay leader who hopes The United Methodist Church's best days might still be ahead. I suspect there will be a new generation of seminary students who will once again whisper to one another between classes, "Have you read Willimon's book yet?" And when they do, like me, they will be inspired, encouraged, and challenged to devote themselves to the task of leading The United Methodist Church to a future with hope.

Bishop Willimon, thank you for your faithful leadership.

Adam Hamilton
Senior Pastor
The United Methodist Church of the Resurrection,
Leawood, KS

INTRODUCTION

She walked off a dearly loved job and, in her early forties, went back to school in an academic field in which she had no previous experience. Her husband and her teenagers vowed never to forgive her for announcing, "God wants me to be a United Methodist minister."

She borrowed fifty thousand dollars to help pay for the education that the church requires, leapt a dozen hurdles, and endured a grueling examination on UM doctrine, history, and polity for the Board of Ordained Ministry and two more years of probation.

All of that has brought her to where she kneels before me in the Service of Ordination. I hold a crosier in one hand and give her a Bible with the other, ominously ordering, "Take authority to preach the word." I ask her to promise loyalty to The United Methodist Church, to defend our doctrine, and, most outrageous of all, to vow submissively to go wherever a bishop like me sends a pastor like her. I then lay hands on her head, praying that the Holy Spirit enable her to do what she has so brashly promised.

Of all episcopal duties, the making of new clergy is the most sacred. I will miss laying on of hands, a revolutionary gesture counter to everything that Americans believe. A vow to subordinate personal ambition, marriage, family, a comfortable income, and even the choice of where to sleep at night to the mission of the Bride of Christ is mind-boggling recklessness. The odds are something like one in four that she will make it no more than ten years as a pastor before she burns out, blacks out, or backs out.

For these eight years I have had the responsibility to stand before new clergy like her, lay hands upon their heads, order them to tell the truth that most of us assiduously avoid, pray for the

Holy Spirit to zap them, and proclaim that their ministry was God's idea before it was theirs. I am unworthy to be here, as I have been unworthily located nearly everywhere Jesus has placed me. As bishop, my joyful job has been to confirm the Holy Spirit's vocational exploits. My hands tremble as I lay them upon their heads.

Ordination's central gesture is the laying on of hands (Greek: *epitithenai tas cheiras*), a symbolic act that was probably derived from rabbinic custom (1 Tim. 4:14; 5:22; 2 Tim. 1:6). Laying on of hands symbolizes: (1) the gift of the Holy Spirit—Christian leadership is too tough to be done alone, and (2) the bestowal of authority by those who have preceded us in ministry—clergy don't have to "reinvent the wheel"; an endless line of splendor shows the way.

UM ministers serve "under appointment" by a bishop. A cardinal principle (in a church without cardinals) is that every pastor serve with supervision and oversight—*episcope*. Methodists believe that clergy should never, ever be left to our own devices. Assisted by the eight district superintendents on my Cabinet, I watch over pastors—all 630 of them—along with their 157,000 sheep who risk Methodism in North Alabama.

Though a host of renewal groups and ecclesiastical whiners disagree, bishops are among the greatest virtues of The United Methodist Church. Our first name, in 1784, was The Methodist *Episcopal* Church (emphasis mine). In the United States our 1787 *Doctrines and Discipline*, at Francis Asbury's urging, substituted the term *bishop* for Wesley's preferred *superintendent*. Thomas Coke, in his sermon at the "ordination" of Francis Asbury as bishop in 1784, after charging that the sorry priests sent by Anglican bishops from the Church of England were "parasites" and the "bottle companions of the rich and the great," joyously proclaimed that "these intolerable fetters are now struck off." Light has dawned; God said, "Let there be Methodist bishops." And though this provoked John Wesley's ire and Charles Wesley's lyrical parody, the term stuck. Our 1808 Constitution says we are free to change many aspects of our life together, but we can never do away with bishops.

I asked a group of new Methodists why they had joined our band. Some liked our friendliness; others our warm, heartfelt worship. To my shock, one woman said, "You are the reason I'm a Methodist." (Which of my books had made her Methodist? I wondered.)

"Never again will I be a member of a church with unsupervised clergy. I've been abused by a succession of arrogant, demagogic preachers who were unaccountable to anybody but us poor laity; never again."

I offered her a job going around with me to tell Methodists how blessed they were to have me.

"What to teach; how to teach; what to do," were the three questions Wesley employed at his first conferences.[1] In previous books I've discussed the first two.[2] This book is of the "what to do" genre. I am one of the fifty North American Methodists who has been summoned to an improbable vocation. (About twenty more bishops serve outside the United States.) For two quadrennia (known in the real world as eight years), I've laid hands on heads, made them promise to go where I send them, overseen their ministries, and acted as if this were normal. Here is my account of what I learned and—more important—what my beloved church must do to have a future as a viable movement of the Holy Spirit.

My friend Russell Richey said, "United Methodists generally exhibit little interest in the actual office of bishop."[3] Insouciance about bishops is probably a sign of right priorities. Yet Russ has said he also believes that bishops are a key to the renewal of our church.[4] Most college professors, writers, and campus ministers—three roles I performed before being bishop—do their jobs in much the same way as they did for the past century. In chess, bishops move diagonally. The diagonal movement of The UMC ministry of oversight has been upward, changing more in the past ten years than in the previous one hundred. In preparation for this work, I've read dozens of books by bishops and about bishops, and I can say that this book couldn't have been written a decade ago. Many things need changing in The United Methodist Church, but the most dramatic change that precedes all the rest has been among some of us bishops.[5]

My way of being bishop is not the only way. By the grace of God and the summons of the church, however, I've had a privileged peek at the inner machinery of the ecclesia, tried some things that work, and made lots of mistakes. In response to my books, weekly blogs, tweets, or podcasts, some urged me, on my way out the door, to share what I've learned. This is my testimony to my fellow United Methodists that though they may be frustrated by the pace of change within their congregation or in the church at large, they may take heart that many bishops have changed.

Everybody knows I've not been the best bishop who ever was. It's easier to be a bishop in a book than in actual practice. Mine is not the final word on the episcopacy (post-Resurrection there are no "final words"; we serve a forward-looking, living God). As Kierkegaard famously said, life can only be understood looking backwards but unfortunately one has to live life forward. Here is my backward look so that we might better understand the forward movement of one of the most curious of the church's ministries.[6] I hope this book offers leadership lessons for anyone called to be a transformative leader. As a preacher, preaching somewhere every Sunday, I'm so accustomed to God (occasionally) taking my paltry homiletical efforts and (miraculously) working them up into someone's gift that I incautiously presume God can do it again with this backward look by a bishop on the way out the door.

For all who wanted me to be a bishop and courageously voted down all those who didn't, for Christians in North Alabama who were stirred to ever greater feats of fidelity while I watched over them in love, this is my gratitude for the opportunity to be a bishop.

And to those who graciously forgave me for once calling UM bishops "the bland leading the bland," thanks.

Will Willimon
Pentecost 2011

CHAPTER ONE

BODY OF CHRIST IN MOTION

It's a typical Sunday morning for Patsy and me. We drive past fallow fall fields, trustworthy GPS coaxing us down rural roadways. Just an hour beyond Birmingham we descend a low hill, autumnal trees part, and we see a little white-frame building that is typecast as everyone's idea of a church. An hour before the service a few pickup trucks are gathered in the church's gravel lot. Spotting an aging Ford parked in the shade, I comment knowledgeably, "The pastor is here."

"This county now has the third highest influx of Spanish-speaking people. That building was built after the fire, in the 1940s. They still call it 'the new church,'" I say, showing off my reading. I ask for a summary of the demographic context and the congregational history when I make a Sunday visit. While my sermon preparation is helped by knowledge of the congregation's past, the sad truth is that most of my congregations have more history behind them than future before them.

Most of our congregations, like the one where I'm the visiting preacher today, were planted a century ago. The community that gave them birth has relocated. Though the people around the congregation have changed, the congregation has remained fixed confined to the same rhythms of congregational life that worked for them decades ago but no longer work today.

That's one of the things people love about a church—it doesn't move. It blooms where planted and, long after it withers, it stays planted. We build our churches to look at least two

1

hundred years older than they are. Inside, the pews are bolted down, heavy and substantial. That the world around the church is chaotic and unstable is further justification for the church to be fixed and final.

One of my younger churches worships in the "contemporary worship" idiom. The pastor complained of boredom: "We are singing the same songs, using the same pattern of worship that we've been stuck with for the past twenty years. Worst of all, we call it *contemporary!*"

"Why not change?" I asked naively.

"This is a mobile suburban neighborhood," he explained. "Only a couple of my members have seniority on me. The last thing my people want is for church to force even more change. Contemporary has become our hallowed, immutable tradition."

In a time when many feel overwhelmed by change—the government's economic attack on the middle class, high unemployment among young adults, shifting political alliances, soaring debt for the world's biggest military, the demise of once-sound institutions, changing social mores, the information explosion—the church is tapped to play the role of immobile island amid a sea of change.

What is incomprehensible is that we call this stability-protecting, past-perpetuating institution "the Body of Christ." All the Gospels present Jesus as a ceaseless peripatetic. Never once did he say, "Settle down with me." No, with vagabond Jesus it was always, "Follow me!"

Consider the first days of Christ's resurrected life. Not content just to be raised from the dead, the risen Christ is in motion, returning to the rag-tag group of Galilean losers who had failed him (Matt. 28:16-20).

And what does Jesus say? "You have had a rough time. Settle down in Galilee among these good country folk with whom you are most comfortable. Buy real estate, build, get a good mortgage, and enjoy being a spiritual club"? No. The risen Christ commands, "Get out of here! Make me disciples, baptizing and teaching everything I've commanded! And don't limit yourselves to Judea. Go to everybody, to undocumented immigrants, everybody! I'll stick with you until the end of time—just to be sure you obey me."

How like the rover Jesus to disallow rest. Refusing to permit disciples to hunker down with their own kind, he sent those who had so disappointed him forth on the most perilous of missions— in Jesus' name, to take back the world that belonged to God. There is no way to be with Jesus, to love Jesus, without obediently venturing with Jesus. "Go! Make disciples!"

The United Methodist Church should rejoice in a new generation of overseers who feel called to administer but also to lead, not simply to manage an ecclesiastical system, but to push, pull, cajole, and threaten that system to become again the Body of Christ in motion. Once bishops were the personification of stability, our link with the past, our assurance that, despite any minor modifications, we were still the same.

Today a growing group of bishops are not simply allowing but also leading change. Their transformative leadership arises from institutional and from theological concerns. Though we have a rapidly shrinking and declining church on our hands, we are also in the hands of a Savior who was crucified because he destabilized the messianic expectations of the faithful and was resurrected and ascended as sign of God's determination not to allow death to have the last word.

LEADING AND MANAGING THE BODY OF CHRIST

Our Service of Consecration for Bishops says succinctly what bishops are for:

You are now called, as bishop in the Church, . . .
to represent Christ's servanthood in a special ministry of
oversight.

3

You are called to guard the faith, to seek the unity,
and to exercise the discipline of the whole Church;
and to supervise and support the Church's life, work,
and mission throughout the world.

As servant of the whole Church,
you are called to preach and teach
the truth of the gospel to all God's people;
to lead the people in worship,
in the celebration of the Sacraments,
and in their mission of witness and service in
the world,
and so participate in the gospel command
to make disciples of all nations. . . .

Your joy will be to follow Jesus the Christ
who came not to be served but to serve.

Will you accept the call to this ministry as bishop
and fulfill this trust in obedience to Christ?[1]

My only cavil is that the service's opening verbs—"guard," "represent," "administer," "supervise," "support"—are not active enough to characterize the work of a new breed of UM bishops. Shove, coax, bargain, and beg are more true to what we bishops now do for the love of God.

To perform "the special ministry of oversight," bishops, like all ministers of the gospel, are called. Jesus Christ gets his movement in motion by vocation, calling a group of ordinary people to help him do the work of the kingdom. His saving work was the communal reconstitution of the scattered lost sheep of Israel, not merely an appeal to a group of isolated individuals. Jesus Christ is God's definitive statement to humanity that God refuses to be God alone. Ever the great delegator, Jesus chooses not to save the world by himself. Thus a bishop's work is rarely solo.

"Loneliness at the top is the worst part of this job," an experienced bishop warned me. He was wrong. The *Discipline* defines bishops as elders who lead a team of elders (the bishop's cabinet) whose primary means of leading the church is through the deployment of a community of pastors (ministerial members of the annual conference) to lead the mission of our congregations and the far-flung ministries of our church.[2]

Not much lonely about that.

Ron Heifetz is right. The greatest "myth of leadership is the myth of the lone warrior."[3] The Cabinet preserves me from this fantasy. The bishop-district superintendent system is a wonderfully team-based, consultative, collegial way of working that offers a maximum of interaction with different perspectives. Information can be unearthed and shared, conflict can be orchestrated, and moves can be interpreted collegially. As Aristotle said, "Feasts to which many contribute excel those provided at one person's expense."[4] The decisions that we made together—and I can't think of a single important decision that was not concerted—were not only better decisions but also ones that had a greater likelihood of being well executed. Never could any member of my Cabinet say of a pastoral appointment, "That appointment was the bishop's idea." Few mistakes were solely mine. Change initiated in North Alabama was never my personal program; the Cabinet contributed, advised, initiated, questioned, criticized, or praised every step along the way.

The most important appointment a bishop makes is the selection of district superintendents; everything hinges upon whom the bishop chooses to manage pastors and churches. A district superintendent (DS) is the glue that holds the connection together, the most active itinerant among itinerating pastors, the administrator of our order and polity, and the main reason we are still able to be an episcopal church. No vision of any bishop has been realized, no episcopal directive is executed without the consent and work of a DS. Nothing moves in The UMC until a DS commits to leading that change.

If you know my past, you know how difficult it is for me to make these laudatory statements about district superintendents. As a product of the antiauthoritarian 1960s, during the first years of ministry I regarded a district superintendent in much the same way as prisoners regard their warden. I've never gotten along well with "A rule is a rule" sort of people. Among the many objections to my being a bishop was, "But you have never even been a DS." My translation: "You lack experience as an unimaginative, rule-enforcing, sycophantic, unctuous bureaucrat."

DSs are now at the apex of my great chain of being, not just because of my experience with DSs while I was an active bishop, but also because of Harvard professor John Kotter's seminal book, *Leading Change*.[5] Leadership and management, said Kotter, are two "distinctive and complementary systems of action." By way of analogy, when Kotter says "leader," were he a Methodist, he would say "bishop" and when he says "manager" I take him to mean "DS."

Though I'm sure that Kotter has heard of neither Bob Wilson nor me, I'm confident that he would agree with our thirty-year-old statement that The UMC is "over managed and under led."[6] Everybody laments the paucity of good leaders. But Kotter warns that strong leadership without good management gets an organization nowhere. While not everyone is both a good manager and a good leader, *effective bishops must be both*. Bishops are leader-managers who lead church managers (DSs) in not only administering but also in beefing up the Body of Christ.

Kotter defines *management* as "coping with complexity." The twentieth century saw the emergence of highly complex, differentiated organizations that easily became chaotic to the point of self-destruction. We have so many different sorts of UM churches—somewhat interconnected—and in so many different places, served by a diversity of pastors, that careful, comprehensive, coherent management is essential. In 1972 we created a form of church where even the lowest reaches of the organization were required to duplicate the complexity of the highest levels. A complex, bureaucratic process of decision-making and governance consumed huge energy. Every congregation, even the weakest, was required to ape the organization of the church at large. DSs were fated to become the most important persons in the system because the system required so much management. The greatest good produced by management, said Kotter, is organizational "order and consistency," which for the 1972 General Conference were more important than practicality and productivity.

Leadership (bishop), unlike management (DS), is not primarily about order and consistency. Leaders administer change. American churches find themselves in a competitive, conflicted environment where mainline Protestantism has lost its monopoly on the practice of Protestant Christianity. A living God gives churches two choices: grow (that is, change) or die (dead doesn't change).

Change cannot be managed; it must be led. Management (district superintendent [DS]) is needed to cope with complexity; leadership (bishop) is needed for change. Management increases an organization's capacity to move forward by organizing and staffing, developing necessary structures, evaluating and planning, holding people accountable, rewarding people who contribute, and exiting people who detract from an institution's forward movement. Leadership (bishop) helps people move in the same general direction by talking—motivating and inspiring.

Management and leadership are companions. We need both DSs and bishops because we are desperate for the fruits of good management and we are dying for lack of inspired leadership. Yet here's the rub for bishops: while DSs need not be great leaders, bishops must perform *both* management and leadership functions.

Leaders help an organization articulate and reiterate a vision. A *leader of change* must not only cultivate and encourage a vision but also do the hard, sweaty, unglamorous management work required to imbed and to instigate that change. I estimate that I spent about 20 percent of my time as a leader and about 80 percent of my time as a manager. Though the 20 percent of me that was a leader was the most consequential part of me for the long-term good of the church, my leadership would have gotten us nowhere without the 80 percent of me as manager—*going to meetings*, selecting the right DSs, reading and responding to reports on ministry, studying the stats for the productivity of pastors and churches, *going to meetings*, evaluating personnel, holding direct reports accountable, and *going to meetings*.

Management values control and devalues risk; leadership requires energy and, therefore, inspiration (literally "filled with spirit"). No grand vision is achieved, said Kotter, without "a burst of energy." Managers push people through mechanisms of oversight and control. Leaders inspire people by energetically playing to people's basic need for achievement, a sense of belonging, recognition by others, and the power to live up to their highest ideals. Thus good leaders tend to be inspiring motivators; they know how to assess people's highest values and they enhance those values. They invite others into decisions and give them a sense that they have some control over their destiny. Leaders discover the organization's most successful leaders and then they attempt to recognize and to reward those people in order to add value to the organization.[7]

Bishops who want to be transformative leaders of change must not become enslaved to their management tasks, but they must manage. Later I will describe my struggle to fulfill both functions in service to a church that must either change (grow) or continue to shrink (die).

Because The United Methodist Church needs changing, one of the essential tasks of a leader like a bishop is to identify, to develop, and to motivate transformative leadership in others, particularly in the DSs. Leadership initiative is needed from people at every level, particularly among the managers. Motivation comes through example and communication. The United Methodist Church is blessed by an established, functioning network of churches known affectionately as "the connection."[8] The connection provides the bishop who is leader-manager with multiple opportunities and means of communicating the need for and the means to change. A DS explains and reiterates change to all the churches, always on the lookout for clergy and laity who appear to "get it."

Nelson Mandela remembered an aged tribal chief's maxim for leadership: "A leader is like a shepherd. He stays behind the flock, letting the most nimble go out ahead, whereupon the others follow, not realizing that all along they are being directed from behind."[9] A bishop, as shepherd, creates space for the most nimble to go ahead, praying that the flock will follow the most nimble rather than lag behind with the sluggish and the fearful.

Persons to be considered for the role of DS need not have been in their clergy careers the greatest preachers, the most learned teachers, or the most caring pastors. They must be leaders who have taken opportunities in their churches for risk-taking in order to produce change and managers who are willing to shoulder the responsibilities of supervision.

Although I managed a large staff and a big budget in my previous job, that contributed little to my leadership. (Academia is notorious for its lack of accountability.) My most significant preparation for being bishop was four years as pastor in a rapidly declining, isolated, demoralized, inner-city congregation. Every transformative leadership skill required to give that congregation a future proved to be wonderfully transferable to my work in *episcope*.

LEADERSHIP IN CONTEXT: ALABAMA

All ministry is a demonstration of the Incarnation; the Trinity refuses to be relegated to the abstract and the detached but rather locates, incarnates, tabernacles among us. My particular experience of Incarnation was, in the wisdom of the Jurisdictional Episcopacy Committee, Alabama. From one angle Alabama is an example of bad state government and a string of sad choices by the voters (many of whom are United Methodists).[10] Where George Wallace stood in a schoolhouse door snarling "segregation now, segregation forever," our current governor (proclaiming himself to be an exemplary Christian) stands in the way of government becoming more responsive to its citizens—one of his few initiatives in his first year was passage of the most

9

mean-spirited anti-immigration legislation in the nation (which the Episcopal and Roman Catholic bishops joined with me in challenging in court). A 2009 Gallup Poll of political ideology found Alabama the most conservative US state.[11] Our economy is utterly dependent on US military largesse.[12] Although our legislators bad-mouth the feds, the US sends Alabama $1.66 for every dollar we pay in federal tax. Alabama stubbornly refuses to elect or even appoint women to public service, having fewer women leading in public life than any state in the Union. We have the most regressive tax system in the country, supported by a racist, labyrinthine constitution that was conceived in sin to protect the economic privilege of white people.[13] Efforts by many United Methodists to lead change in our constitution and our tax structure have been continually rebuffed, often by better-financed right-wing Christians (some of whom are United Methodists). We are one of the most polluted states in the country. The Birmingham mayor is now serving a long prison sentence for stealing huge sums from the people. "God knows what I have done and not done, and that's enough for me," Mayor Langford said on his way to jail, "Everybody else can go to hell."

And yet by the grace of God, Alabama is also the home of Helen Keller and Rosa Parks. The state that called itself "The Heart of Dixie," is also where Martin Luther King, Jr. was discovered, where Booker T. Washington and George Washington Carver worked, where Methodist Harper Lee wrote our nation's finest novel, and where lots of courageous Methodists dismantled racial segregation.

In 1921 a Methodist preacher (also an active member of the KKK) shot dead Father James Coyle for marrying his daughter to a Puerto Rican, was acquitted, and continued to preach the gospel.[14] Alabama was the national center for religious terrorism, with nearly two dozen bombs planted in churches and synagogues between 1949 and 1965.[15] Alabama has the largest percentage of citizens in church on a Sunday and the second most generous individual givers in the nation.[16] Make of that what you will.

10

You would have to be a Christian to understand why Patsy and I considered it a great privilege to be assigned to serve God in 'Bama. For one thing, being beset by legions of biblical literalists, neo-Calvinist fundamentalists, and Baptist bigots is a golden opportunity to rediscover the vitality and intellectual superiority of Wesleyan Christianity. I always loved our theological heritage, but Alabama taught me the continuing glorious human implications of Arminianism in action. Time and again, in a sob session of criticism of our UM problems, there was always someone to say, "It took me thirty years to find The United Methodist Church and I love it! I never heard of grace until I met Methodists."

For another thing, Alabama is partly in a fix due to our propensity to choose leaders who exemplify the worst in us. And I'm not just talking about the current legislature. All of which means that Methodist Alabamians were wonderfully responsive to leadership inspired by Christ rather than by mean-spirited, self-interested resentment. My prayer sessions with our former governor, Bob Riley, gave me a glimpse into the huge challenges faced by a consecrated Christian leader and almost converted me into voting Republican. Almost.

Sure, it's sad that Alabama stays forty-eighth in factors relating to childhood health, education, and safety.[17] However, the plight of poor children in our state was one reason Patsy committed so much time and effort to our thriving, excellent network of UM Children's Homes in Alabama.

I suppose there are places in the world where churches thrash about trying to find something courageous to do. Not in Alabama. Having one of the most irresponsible and corrupt governments in the country gives us a God-ordained opportunity to reach out to those in need in the name of Jesus Christ. My high regard for my courageous clergy who dare to speak out and act up for Jesus in Alabama is unbounded.

"If some teenager is to be rescued, if a crack mom is to be saved in this county, The United Methodist Church is the only organized, caring way that's to be done," said one of my preachers. Her church promised God that although Alabama has found so many ways to ignore the poor, The United Methodist Church will not.

In my better moments, when I became discouraged by the reactionary attitudes of some of our people, God would graciously remind me that Alabama has one of the worst school systems in America, kept down by a self-protective state teachers' association and underfunded by the nation's most regressive tax system. I would see our situation as a call for better Christian teaching, not for more moralistic scolding, and thank God I got to serve God in Alabama.

Whenever I encountered resistance, I remembered the words of Martin Luther King, Jr., when he was told to ease up on Alabama. In his sermon, "Our God is Marching On," King vowed, "No, we will not allow Alabama to return to normalcy."

Normalcy ceased to be an option for The United Methodist Church in Alabama once I got my books unpacked and reported for service as 'Bama Bishop.

CHAPTER TWO

SUMMONED TO BE BISHOP

Ordination is a gift of God to the church.
—The United Methodist Service of Ordination

Many who knew me reacted to my call to the episcopacy with incomprehension. "You will be miserable," more than one predicted. A seminary dean declared, "You will be bored to tears, spending so much time with so many mediocre clergy."

To say, "You are ill equipped for the tasks of ministry, most of which are futile and archaic" and "You could be happier in another line of work with higher social status" is a waste of words to a Methodist preacher and suggests that the critic has little understanding of the peculiar nature of Christian vocation. Of course, I was poorly endowed with gifts for the episcopacy. I admit that I could have enjoyed many other human undertakings easier than the episcopacy—professional football coaching and university presidency leap to mind.

Ministry, in any of its forms, is always God's idea before it is ours. While we may eventually enjoy our clerical vocation, we do it first of all not because it causes us bliss but rather because it is the job to which God has called us. Jesus loves to summon odd people to painful, impossible tasks—read the Bible.

All Christian leadership begins in God's determination to have a people in motion helping God retake what is God's. For we who oversee the ministry of our church, sometimes the great challenge is to believe in the church half as much as God in Christ believes in us, though laity can be forgiven for watching us pastors and bishops in action and thinking lots before thinking "gift of God."

Nan Keohane defines leadership as "providing solutions to common problems or offering ideas about how to accomplish collective purposes, and mobilizing the energies of others to follow those courses of action."[1] This is as good a global definition of leadership as I know—except for one missing element—*God*. A bishop allows God the Father to define our common problems, asking Jesus Christ for the grace to find solutions that are compatible with the Christian view of reality, and then assists the Holy Spirit in mobilizing the energies of fellow disciples to do the work. All Christian leadership is under obligation to keep our leadership theological rather than lapse into a-theism (attempting to lead as if God were not).

When Rowan Williams was made Archbishop of Canterbury, the press asked if he had doubts: "You'd be a maniac not to have doubts . . ." he replied. "It's a job that inevitably carries huge expectations and projections . . . other people's fantasies . . . and to try and keep some degree of honesty, clarity and simplicity in the middle of that is going to be hard work—so that frightened me a lot."[2] Fear and trembling accompany the summons to the ministry of oversight, fear of God's demands, apprehension of the church's fantasies and expectations, dread of your own limits. Considering our present obsession with leadership, it's odd that the New Testament has little to say on the subject. Scripture seldom bothers with bishops:

> Now a bishop must be worthy of reproach, the husband of one wife, temperate, sensible, dignified, hospitable, an apt teacher, no drunkard, not violent but gentle, not quarrelsome, and no lover of money. (1 Tim. 3:2-3)

Well, at least I am the husband of one wife.

While I take comfort that First Timothy has modest ethical expectations for bishops, these days it isn't easy being bishop. The bishop of Rome continues to twist in the wind due to almost daily revelations of sex abuse by priests under his care. The archbishop of the Church of England isn't doing so hot either. Though I'm far from the depth of his intellect, like Rowan I came to the episcopacy from academia and, like him, have difficulty being comprehended. I am also an antiestablishmentarian now forced to prop up and to defend the establishment. And like the good archbishop, I can't find a way fully to please either conservatives or liberals, much less to tell the difference between them.

Yet I have been summoned, and so I must lead.

THE MINISTRY OF OVERSIGHT

The church of any era is a mess, though our current mess has a particular character. From the first the church has had dissonance with every culture in which we found ourselves. My first month as bishop I reread Gregory the Great's *Pastoral Care*, Gregory's eloquent argument for why he never under any circumstances should be bishop.[3] Read in tandem with John Chrysostom's *On the Priesthood*, it is a great guide for a bishop. In the Early Middle Ages it was custom to place Gregory's book into the hands of bishops at their consecration. (An irony of the episcopacy is that those who are most reluctant to be bishop are the ones who ought to bear this burden. The historic test to be a bishop was to be able to say, "*Nolo episcopare*," "I don't want to be a bishop.")

Gregory would bar anyone "with a little nose" from being bishop, "for by the nose we discern sweet odors from stench."[4] Let all bishops pray for big noses.

On my way to Alabama to be bishop I had a stomach-churning call from my predecessor detailing a sordid clergy misconduct case that he was handing off to me on his way out. "Was there penetration? How many assignations did you have?" he had asked the alleged perpetrator. Though my mother would disapprove of my engaging in such conversation, I give thanks that I'm from the South, where we still believe in sin, rather than from someplace sentimental, where human culpability is a surprise.

15

In my book on clergy ethics, I roundly criticized the church for sometimes sweeping clerical sins under the rug.[5] Between then and now I inherited a conference where abuse cases are handled openly, swiftly, and justly. By meeting with the alleged victim, sitting across from someone who has come to the church in her time of need only to be used by an unfaithful clergyman for his own gratification gives me the courage to say, "I love being a Methodist preacher and don't want someone like you to spoil our vocation for the rest of us. Adios."

My conference requires extensive ministerial integrity training for all our pastors, but Barbara Blodgett said nothing is more effective in curtailing sexual misconduct than for those at the top to deal with clergy moral lapses swiftly and openly.[6] The ten minutes it took me to remove two of my DSs from the ministry because of their violation of their marital covenants did more for clergy integrity than weeks of workshops.

The word *bishop* (*episcopos*) means simply "overseer." It's a wonderfully functional and mundane designation. For the church to work, somebody has got to oversee. Bishops don't fix everything that's wrong or do everything that needs doing. We simply watch over Christ's property, his Body, the church.

There are days when I wish I could make more vaunted claims for my *episcope*.

"Why must you pack up and move family, pets, and library from Brown Swamp to Dismal Prospect? Because I said so. Remember, as a bishop I stand in the unbroken line of apostolic succession."

Assertions of apostolic continuity, though historically cherished by much of the church, are weak rationale for episcopal authority. Methodism didn't begin with an intention to have bishops—Wesley initiated a lay renewal movement in the Church of England that already had bishops, many of whom didn't care for John Wesley. The feeling was mutual. But in America, Wesley's "poor sheep in the wilderness" needed new pastors, and when the Church of England failed to respond, Francis Asbury and Thomas Coke took it upon themselves to be bishops, with Wesley's later begrudging acquiescence.[7]

From the earliest days of the People Called Methodist, the notion that sanctificationist-perfectionist-evangelical Wesleyans should have bishops has been contested (first by Wesley). In 1787 at the South Carolina Annual Conference (my native Conference), Asbury, without much explanation or consultation, changed the title "superintendent" to "bishop."

Bishops for Methodists in America were an embarrassment for Wesley. Our Old Daddy, as he was frequently called (sometimes with sarcasm, sometimes in affection) had always attempted to reassure critical Anglicans that he was not attempting ecclesial schism and that his "superintendents" in no way usurped the role of bishops of the Church of England.

"How can you dare suffer yourself to be called Bishop?" Wesley wrote his "dear Franky."[8]

"I shudder at the very thought!" Wesley railed. "Men may call me a knave or a fool, a rascal, a scoundrel, and I am content; but they shall never by my consent call me Bishop! [ouch!] . . . for Christ's sake put an end to this!" It was the last letter Asbury received from Wesley.

In defense of a Methodist episcopacy, Thomas Coke said, "Of all the forms of church government, we think *a moderate* episcopacy the best. The executive power being lodged in the hands of one, or at least a few, vigor and activity are given in the resolves of the body, and those two essential requisites for any grand undertaking are sweetly united—calmness and wisdom in deliberating, and in the executive department, expedition and force."[9] There is an episcopacy with checks and balances, not a monarchial episcopate, *episcope* designed to give a young church "expedition and force." In Coke's view, bishops add to the church's resolutions, "vigor and activity"—a revolutionary rationale for bishops.

Asbury spent the rest of his ministry defending and shoring up the notion of a Methodist episcopacy. He fumed about the "growing evil of locality in bishops, elders, preachers, or Conferences," and saw the practice of bishops itinerating throughout the connection as a safeguard against dreaded "locality." (Few sins were more serious for Asbury than for Methodist preachers to grow soft, settle down, give up traveling, and take the easy way out: "location.")

In Asbury's Valedictory Address of 1803 he laboriously, and revealingly, championed two themes: itinerant ministry and the apostolic authority of bishops. He regarded bishops as being "apostolic" to the degree that they itinerate, even making the astounding claim that "the apostolic order of things was lost in the first century" not because of doctrinal lapses but rather because early bishops abandoned itinerancy! Asbury sneered, "There were no local bishops until the second century. Those who were ordained in the second century mistook their calling when they became local and should have followed those bright examples of the apostolic age," saintly itinerating (according to Asbury) bishops like Paul, Barnabas, and Timothy, who were constantly in motion among dozens of congregations. The Reformation did little to end the "rubbish" and "absurdity" of located bishops and thus the episcopacy languished until the heavens opened, a dove descended, and God finally sent the itinerating American Methodists: "In 1784, an apostolic form of Church government was formed in the United States of America at the first General Conference of the Methodist Episcopal Church." Methodism's phenomenal numbers since then convinced Asbury that the itinerating episcopacy was even more sanctified than he had first thought.[10]

Far from being embarrassed by Asbury's actions in the creation of a distinctively Wesleyan general (that is, serving all over the connection), itinerating episcopacy, I treasure our episcopal history. My church has bishops because they were needed to get the job done. Methodism didn't begin as a church with a mission; we are a mission. In the 1798 *Discipline* Asbury and Coke claim that our episcopacy—in its stress on the episcopacy as an instrument of mission—is a revolt from the adulterated Anglican monarchial episcopacy and a recovery of the apostolic pattern. First the task assigned by Christ; then organization and structure cobbled together in order to be faithful to Christ's commission. Bishops are Wesley's "practical divinity," either at its pragmatic best or its historical and theological worst, depending on your theology of the church.

Leroy Long, comparing UM bishops with other episcopal polities, called us a "managerial episcopacy" as opposed to the "monarchial episcopacy" (Roman Catholic) or "pastoral episcopacy" (Episcopal Church). A managerial episcopacy, said Long, "is concerned primarily with making the church function effectively. It views the office of bishop in functional terms, as involving managerial skills, rather than giving it theological dimensions or sacerdotal significance."[11] Long, in Wesleyan Christianity words like *functional*, *managerial*, and *effective* are "theological" and "sacerdotal."

Because I'm a Wesleyan I believe that all church leadership, bishops or otherwise, is best rationalized on utility rather than by puffed-up theological warrant. Like Luther, I prefer a pragmatic rather than an ontological definition of pastors; claim too much theological chrism for the ordained *cleros* and next thing you know you have damaged the baptismally bestowed ministry of the *laos*. That's why I personally don't like the relatively recent practice of UM bishops sporting lapel pins with the "Episcopal Seal," purple clergy shirts, pectoral crosses, episcopal rings, and other adopted regalia. Wesleyans taking on airs. I suspect that UM bishops don these superficial accoutrements for the same reason that Methodist pastors began wearing robes in the last century—we need protective clothing while doing hard work and speaking tough truth. I admit that I have days when I wish for a bishop's miter, crosier, and cope, and a white, armored Popemobile; surely these would give me clout I do not otherwise have.

One unintended blessing of a hierarchical ecclesiastical system is the luxury of being able to blame people at the top for anything objectionable in the system. Nearly all of American Methodism's declensions in the past two hundred years, from O'Kelly's defection onward, have had as one of their chief sources good old American democratic antipathy toward bishops. Perhaps that's why recent General Conferences have taken every opportunity to divest power from our bishops—"hierarchy bad, democracy good" is the reasoning. Episcopal we may be in polity, but good old American populism rules in much of our practice. Many of the things that bishops once did for the church are now assigned to bureaucrats, boards, and agencies. No one thinks that our bureaucratic Methodist curia has improved the way the church works. When General Conference was recently asked to allow bishops to chair legislative committees, an insidious power play by the bishops was suspected. (Bishops didn't relish wasting time on pointless legislative committees anyway.) The laborious, dysfunctional, preposterous, General Conference legislative logjam continued unabated. So there.

When I was elected bishop, I lost vote and voice at any annual, jurisdictional, or General Conference. Every four years, the few bishops who are trusted by their colleagues not to cause trouble on the podium get to preside at General Conference while the rest of us lounge on stage silent and bored, as useless as tonsils. Renewal buddies from Good News, the Confessing Movement, and the infamous Institute on Religion and Democracy complain, "You bishops must step up and more courageously lead the church." These are the same evangelical whiners who have jumped at every opportunity to render bishops into smiling, silent ciphers. Our present church finds itself beset by a host of seemingly intractable problems that will never be solved by a committee or a thousand-member meeting. We have a string of difficult decisions that desperately need to be made and are bereft of executive leadership to make them. Serves 'em right.[12]

Reluctance to give bishops authority and agency, coupled with a plea for bishops to lead, could be a good thing. My leadership mentor, Ron Heifetz of Harvard, said that it's disastrous for a leader to confuse authority to lead (formal authorization, legislated power) with leadership (power to question, to teach, to build consensus, and to motivate).

Thus, bishops are not only a sign of the unity of the church but also of peculiar Christian authority. Without defining what it's talking about, the *Discipline* calls us "servant leaders" (404.1). I define the service of bishops as an eagerness to undertake those tasks that the church needs doing in our time and place as the church.

At the same time, in a bishop's appointment of pastors, in our caring for the order of the churches and their accountability, and in our occasional disciplining of the pastors, we are top-down, authoritarian hierarchy personified—and there is plenty of biblical support for that. In us bishops, The United Methodist Church continues to be a mix of Holy Spirit-bottom-up popular consensus and democratic power sharing alongside Holy Spirit-top-down obedience so risky that it requires hierarchical prodding and pushing.

The United Methodist Church is a participatory democracy, sort of. Even though I personally enjoy living in the United States, a liberal democracy, I find little support in Scripture for democratic practices. The unproductive, deleterious, leaden pace of General Conference is perilously close to the California Senate.

Quaker meetings refer to "weightier friends" among an essentially egalitarian gathering of friends. Bishops bear a similarly bestowed authority. I'm an elder who plays a role in service to the church. When someone says, "You are a decisive leader," they are commenting on the office I'm fulfilling, not assessing my personality. And when someone says, as my Episcopal Committee said to me, "Sometimes you are too abrasive," they may mean, "You are serving the church by pushing us to do painful work that we have been avoiding for decades."

The Peculiarity of Christian Leadership

Leaders in the church are subordinate to the mission of the church. That's why it's sad that although our *Discipline* begins with wonderful sections on UM theology, history, and doctrine, most of our energy in the last decades has been expended in tinkering with the sections on structure and process. A bishop could now declare (as at least one has) that the Resurrection is hooey and suffer less censure than if he had questioned the wisdom of forming the membership of every committee by quotas for gender, ethnic, geographical, and clerical/lay representation.

And when the *Discipline* discusses clergy, it expends most of its effort defining who can and can't be clergy and a byzantine process for approving or removing clergy but shows little interest in defining what clergy are for. What are reasonable expectations for the performance of clergy? What do effective clergy produce? We have long lists describing the qualities of clergy with little clarity on what sort of fruitfulness we ought to expect at this time and place in our movement. How very "un-Wesleyan."

By the second century, some churches were led by "bishops" (*episcopoi*, "overseers," "supervisors," sometimes translated "pastors"). In other churches, there seems to have been a council of "elders" (*presbuteroi*) with different elders assuming different duties in the congregation. Eventually, these two patterns must have merged into one, in which bishops presided over a number of congregations with elders becoming pastors or priests of individual churches.[13] This is a key to understanding bishops. Whereas most clergy focus upon the needs of a congregation, bishops care for many congregations—indeed, the church as a whole. Thus from the early days bishops were "big picture" leaders and signs of the unity of the whole Body of Christ even amid a diversity of congregations.

To put it in decidedly Wesleyan terms, bishops signal the church as connection. From the first, American Methodists identified themselves as those who were "in connection with Mr. Wesley." Connectionalism continues to be not only one of The United Methodist Church's defining practices but also compared with most North American Christianity, our most countercultural.[14]

Connectionalism is opposed to congregationalism in our congregations and to individual free agency among our preachers. Bishops are the most vivid representation of our faith in connectionalism. Because all of our congregations are held in trust by The UMC, a bishop and cabinet major in property matters (in trust to the Methodists who sacrificed and produced our churches) and because all of our pastors are members, not of a church but of the connection, bishops also oversee all pastors.

In Hippolytus's second-century account of the ordination of a bishop (which formed the basis of my Duke courses in liturgical history and theology), we detect a core liturgical act that designates bishops: a prayer for the Holy Spirit (*epiclesis*) shows that, though the community chooses, ministry is dependent upon the intervention of God. Little is said in the earliest ordination rites about alleged special characteristics of the clergy; rather, the church needs leadership, and through God and the church, leadership is graciously bestowed by the Holy Spirit and recognized and received by the church. A church with too few leaders is a church that is insufficiently open to the movements of and the designation by the Holy Spirit.

The free movement of the Holy Spirit is one reason it is so difficult for our Boards of Ordained Ministry to make decisions about the fitness of candidates for the ministry. Scripture is full of instances of God calling unbalanced, not-too-bright, ill-equipped, and even disreputable people to positions of leadership in the People of God. After being so often surprised by the Holy Spirit's ability to do some great things through some—in my humble opinion—less-than-great persons, there's a sense in which I know less today about the qualifications for a pastor than I knew eight years ago.

One of my friends, in trying to talk me out of offering myself for the episcopacy, scoffed that, "Bishops are nothing but sanctified personnel managers." It's not an unfair definition of the episcopacy. Leadership is not optional for the church. The Acts of the Apostles tells the story of the first churches mainly through a narrative of the church's leaders. Fidelity in the church won't happen without Spirit-induced leaders and Spirit-filled leaders, and (at least in churches with an episcopal polity) that doesn't happen without bishops.

First Timothy 3:5 says that the overall function of *episcopoi* is "take care of God's church." By the second century, bishops presided at ordinations. It was not until Pope Innocent III (1198-1216) that priests were formally defined as persons who had experienced the rite of laying on of hands "by a duly consecrated bishop." To my Protestant mind, this too closely aligned the authority of pastors with the bestowal of authority by bishops—making it sound as if the authority of a bishop were more significant in making pastors than the call of God and the church. In ordination the bishop signifies and recognizes the call of God and the call of the church in summoning a new generation of clergy, but bishops don't, *ex opera operato,* make clergy.

Unlike bishops in some traditional episcopal churches, bishops in The United Methodist Church have little say in the matter of who does or does not become ordained and whether or not the newly ordained are deployed in the church. Sometimes I chafe at this exclusion. When I was forced to remove a pastor by August after I had laid hands on his head in June, I made some major changes in the Board of Ordained Ministry (or BOOM, the body that oversees the process of making new clergy and the removal of errant clergy and the only body for which I nominate members to the annual conference). It's rather odd that bishops have so little input into the process of selecting clergy, other than nomination of the members of BOOM. I insisted on interviewing each of the persons whom BOOM approved for ordination. I also asked each of them the ordination questions, having a discussion with them about their responses, before we came to the Service of Ordination.

Everybody laments the quality of today's seminarians, alleging a noticeable decline. However, from what I can see as a bishop, Jesus continues to call just the right people into pastoral leadership. The challenge is that even though God calls into ministry, the church must also call. Many Boards of Ordained Ministry lack the boldness and the creativity of the Holy Spirit and the clarity of commitment to the mission of the church, preferring to approve clones of themselves rather than to take a risk on more creative candidates. In order to keep a system static, select people who follow instructions, preserve rigid rules, keep information sharing to a minimum, and develop a clergy selection system that privileges experience and credentials over God-given talent and sacrifices creativity for conformity. That too few churches and pastors notice and encourage their best and brightest to be pastors is a testimonial to the low regard that many clergy have for the vocation to which they have given their lives and to the low expectations many congregations have for their future.

A key to exacting, bold decisions about future clergy is for the board to be very clear about the purpose of clergy in today's UMC. Once our board defined that what we needed from our new clergy was leadership in growth of the church, the rest was easy. For instance, many say, "You can never raise the standards for new clergy as long as the district board is the door into the system. They just can't make negative judgments about hometown kids." We retrained our district boards and clarified with them what sort of new clergy we needed. In the first year they turned down or terminated sixteen candidates. The conference board also ended candidacy for a half dozen of those who had been in process, some of whom had just graduated from seminary, telling them, "We regret that this decision was not made sooner by our board. But we are doing you and the church a favor by making it now. We are not going to be held hostage by the inability of previous Boards of Ministry to make tough decisions."

When churches complain about the quality of clergy sent to them, I ask, "How many talented young people has your congregation (our exclusive source for clergy) sent into the ministry?"

I'm proud to have overseen the complete overhaul of our Board of Ordained Ministry. It's the board's job to decide what sort of pastoral leaders our church now needs and then to use any means at their disposal to figure out if a candidate shows evidence of future fruitfulness. If I were declared King of The United Methodist Church (which may happen any day), I would junk the *Discipline's* boring pages of rules and regulations for ordination in favor of having a dozen of our best clergy thoroughly get to know candidates for the ministry and then make a judgment on whether we want any of them to join our conference.

Most of what our church really needs from its clergy—ideas, commitment to high standards, trust—cannot be had through rules. Or as Saint Paul put it, "The letter [of the law] kills, but the Spirit gives life" (2 Cor. 3:6).

Alas, the paragraphs on ministry in the *Discipline* were concocted by people of my generation (the 1960s), who believe that if there's something worth doing it's necessary to pass a rule to force everyone else to do it. Want better clergy? Get the credentials right: pages of rules, lists of ideal qualities, years of hurdles.

It didn't work. We got a system that's prejudiced toward uncreative bean counters and produces a rapidly rising median age for clergy, when what we desperately need are clergy who are youthful, fruitful, supple, visionary risk-takers. Most of our BOOMs act as if their job is finding people who are good at writing term papers that are handed in on time. Who cares?

I recruited a board with clergy who were exemplars of high expectations for their own ministry and laity with personnel experience. I challenged them to move from a fulfill-all-these-requirements mode to a recruitment mode that says, "We're looking for a few good people to inspire and to lead our churches in North Alabama. Might God have equipped you to enable us to get better results?"

The board had been asking candidates vague questions like "What are your gifts and graces for ministry?"

Surprise. All claimed to possess extraordinary gifts.

Now, seeking transformative leaders, the board asks, "When have you begun a new ministry? Tell us what you did and what you learned from that start-up experience." Or, "Tell us about your most recent failure in leading a church group." No failures suffered, no risks ventured.

I learned that changing personnel on the Cabinet and in the BOOM is the quickest, surest way to change a system. The Cabinet and BOOM that a new bishop inherits will probably need changing if the bishop wants to change the conference culture—present people have produced the present dilemma. Different personnel are required for different results.

Thus the bishop has much the same challenge as that faced by the board in its gatekeeping functions—identifying and recruiting persons whom God has given gifts and graces to lead us into a different future and then encouraging them to lead where God is calling us to go. One of my core beliefs is that God has given us all we need to have a different future than the morbid one to which I once feared we were fated. God gives the church all we need to be faithful. What's lacking are leaders with the wisdom and the courage to call forth and to authorize those clergy and lay leaders who have gifts for transformative leadership.

My greatest contribution in leading change was, in the words of a DS, "to encourage us to do what we knew we should have been doing all along but didn't feel we had permission to do."

There are powerful forces at work to keep the same people in place, doing the same things that they are comfortable doing, and thus getting the same results we've always gotten. Of all my shortcomings, some on my Episcopacy Committee repeatedly criticized me only for moving too fast and for offending some of our old guard clergy (few laity were offended by my leadership). The committee should have complained that I was moving too slowly and that I was attempting to coax the church into a new world while retaining too many power brokers from the old.

An effective pastor's best gift is calling forth new leadership in a congregation, then taking delight in the way that God calls unlikely people to do extraordinary work for God. When I arrived in Alabama, I said that I had personally never attended a session of annual conference that wasn't spiritually debilitating. I was hopeful that our annual meetings didn't have to be defeating, but I wasn't sure of how to make that happen.

One of our youngest staff members stepped up and asked, "Would you like me to show you how to have a more efficient, inspiring, and productive annual conference?"

She had taken it upon herself to keep a log of the previous annual conference.

"Last year we spent nearly fifty minutes waiting for people to walk to the microphone to speak," she noted.

What? Eight hundred people sit waiting for people to stagger to the microphone?

As a thirty-something, she and her buddies have little patience with protracted, unproductive meetings. They transformed our annual conference from a four-day somnambulant conclave to a lively two-day teaching/mission fest. And all I did was simply to say, "Go ahead. Let's see what God may do through you."

One of our real challenges in calling a new generation of pastoral leaders is that too many of our seminaries continue the dated practice of producing people who are good at maintenance but have few skills in growing, transforming, challenging, moving, initiating, and risk-taking.[15] As Bishop Al Gwinn put it, "Our seminaries, at their best, continue to crank out people to care for healthy congregations—which means that they have few gifts for leading 80 percent of our churches!"

We have given seminaries a monopoly (with no accountability) to prepare our pastors, requiring an M.Div. degree for ordination as an elder. Do we know that the possession of an M.Div. degree is requisite for fruitful Christian leadership? It's unrealistic to expect tenured seminary faculty to train risk-taking pastoral leaders; professors tend to value job security and stability and are more attached to their academic field than to the church that funds them. Academia is infected with a studied refusal to take responsibility for the fruit of its labors. As a once tenured seminary professor, I know not to ask the seminaries to give training in the practical skills required to creatively lead a congregation. That's the job of the annual conference.

I take a classical view of seminary education—a seminary's job is to teach the classical ministerial disciplines of biblical interpretation, sermon preparation, theological discernment, church history, Christian theology, liturgical theology, counseling protocol, and biblical languages. A seminary is literally a "seedbed" in which the seeds are planted that bear fruit in later ministry. The church ought to prepare the new minister for the leadership skills that are required to produce fruit in the church in the present age. We thus created a residency in ministry program to redeem the two-year probationary period by pairing new pastors with competent, proven, exemplary pastors who ask, "How can we equip you to do what the church needs doing now?"

We asked master new church planter Paul Borden, "What characteristics do you look for in selecting pastors to start new churches?" We thought Borden would list personality traits or psychological profiles or specify necessary previous experiences. Instead he replied, "A robust belief in the Trinity—people have got to know that God is real and on the move, and a clear Chalcedonian faith—new church pastors must be convinced of a relational, incarnational God." It was a joy to see leadership defined by theological commitments.

It's good for bishops to believe that they have what it takes to lead the church in this time and place; more important for us to believe that a relentless, restless, reaching Trinity has what it takes. The only good reason for anybody to be in ministry is theological.

Thus most of the questions that I ask ordinands from the historic examination are about God:

Do you believe in the Triune God, Father, Son, and Holy Spirit and confess Jesus Christ as your Lord and Savior?

Are you persuaded

that the Scriptures of the Old and New Testaments
contain all things necessary for salvation through faith in
Jesus Christ
and are the unique and authoritative standard?

Will you be faithful in prayer,
in the study of the Holy Scriptures,
and with the help of the Holy Spirit
continually rekindle the gift of God that is in you?

Will you do your best to pattern your life
in accordance with the teachings of Christ?
Will you, in the exercise of your ministry,
lead the people of God to faith in Jesus Christ,
to participate in the life and work of the community, and
to seek peace, justice, and freedom for all people?

Will you be loyal to The United Methodist Church,
accepting its order, liturgy, doctrine, and discipline,
defending it against all doctrines contrary to God's Holy
Word,
and committing yourself to be accountable with those serving
with you,
and to the bishop and those who are?

Dear reader, please note how this examination culminates—with stress on accountability "to the bishop."[16]

In swearing to be answerable to the bishop, ordinands hand me my most daunting duty—accounting for the 630 clergy under my care.

CHAPTER THREE

BISHOPS SENDING PASTORS

Maria writes Malvolio in *Twelfth Night*: "Some are born to leadership; some achieve leadership; others have leadership thrust upon them."[1] Bishops join all clergy in Maria's last category—we are leaders not because of innate qualities or personal preferences but because we were summoned by God and the church and given a job to do for Jesus. United Methodism practices a "sent ministry"; you can't call or hire a UM pastor—we are sent. Ministry is God's idea before it is our own; God has seen fit, for reasons usually known only to God, to thrust us into the mission of the Body of Christ in motion.

One of my goals was to improve the process of sending pastors. Bishops make poor decisions in the sending of pastors because of three deficiencies: lack of accurate information, lack of creativity, and lack of courage. It is our responsibility to know pastors and churches down deep. It's the Holy Spirit's responsibility to give us the guts to act upon that knowledge.

There was a time when some people thought the purpose of a Cabinet was to care for the career advancement of the clergy. Not according to our *Discipline* and not in the North Alabama Conference. I urged our Cabinet to define our work in this way: *The task of the bishop and DSs in the appointive process is to send clergy who can lead the mission of a congregation.*[2]

In an early meeting with some of our clergy couples I was asked if I would do better than my predecessor in appointing clergy couples to desirable appointments. They were asking, whether they intended or not, that the church function for the benefit of clergy. I replied that our system is too clericalized already. Clericalism is always deadly to the church. It's not my job to appoint clergy couples; I secure effective pastoral leadership. When bishops are asked to appoint clergy by criteria other than effectiveness in leading a congregation, we get the lousy results that we deserve.

It is death to a clergy appointment for a bishop when asked by a congregation, "Why have you appointed this pastor to us?" to then respond, "Because her husband is a pastor nearby and we were forced to appoint her within a thirty-mile radius of him." Instead, what a joy to look a congregation in the eye and answer, "Because she is the very best person we have to lead the mission of this particular church."

Good appointments require interplay of assessment of congregational need and pastoral competence. Patsy and I led mission trips with young pastors and spouses both to teach that mission engagement is a key to long-term vitality in ministry and to get deep knowledge of new personnel.[3] When visiting in a congregation, I asked to have Sunday dinner with key lay leadership, asking them a series of questions about activity within the congregation in order better to know my churches. The most revealing indicator of congregational vitality is the trend in worship attendance—how many United Methodist Christians will get out of bed on a Sunday and worship God under that pastor's leadership? Other important indicators of vitality are baptisms, new members, hands-on mission engagement, and, especially, professions of faith.

We ask all our churches to take the Natural Church Development (NCD) congregational inventory.[4] Understanding a church's greatest barrier to growth (Minimum Factor) and its strength for growth (Maximum Factor) gives a district superintendent insight to determine if the current pastoral leadership is capable of leading a church forward. We use NCD results in our conversations with congregations about pastoral appointments, finding it a helpful means of sticking with the facts and keeping the focus upon the mission of the congregation.

Of course, the best way to assess the health and the well-being of a church is through direct observation as DSs engage the church through visits, interaction via e-mail, phone calls, or at training events and through prayer. Less than 12 percent of our churches experience a pastoral change in a given year (the national average is about 30 percent), indicative of our move toward longer pastorates. My first year, at our first session in the spring to discuss possible upcoming appointments, one hundred pastors stated they would like to be moved. (Most requests for a move come from the pastor rather than the congregation.) Back then we asked each pastor and congregation to complete a questionnaire in the winter, checking off whether or not the pastor desired to stay, to move, or was open to a move.

That first year we had a number of deep salary cuts for the first pastors whom we decided to move—cuts due to shrinking congregational resources because of shrinking membership. Overnight 150 projected moves shrank to 100. Obviously, pastors were attempting to manipulate the appointive process to fish for a better-paying appointment, moving for a prospect of a higher salary, if not, hunkering down for another year. There are good reasons for a pastor moving or staying; none have to do with a pastor's salary advancement.

Never again would we use the preference sheets. Those sheets put in pastors' minds that the solution to some problem in their leadership was simply to head for another congregation where they would be preserved from having to grow and get better. Also, when the system is driven by "I might like to move this year," it is easy for a congregation to be infected with the usually erroneous notion, "There is nothing wrong with this church that can't be cured by getting rid of this pastor, so we won't have to face our sickness, and we can continue believing that the problems in this church are because of the pastor."

One of our slogans: *The Cabinet and bishop not only make appointments, we help make appointments work.*

MAKING GOOD DECISIONS ABOUT CLERGY DEPLOYMENT

Sometimes pastors initiated a move because they felt they had accomplished their main goals. At other times they requested a move because they had reached an impasse with the congregation. Often the DS urged the pastor and congregation to work through their impasse, to dig in and pray for transformation of the congregation. A DS must work with a congregation to keep judgments about pastors focused on a pastor's actual leadership of congregational mission. When a pastor asked to be moved, we insisted that the pastor be honest with the congregation. A church needs to know that its pastor has been sent to them for a time and will eventually move to another season of ministry elsewhere. Too many of our unhealthy congregations delude themselves into thinking that they are a joy for pastors to serve and that there is nothing wrong with them that can't be cured by the sending of a pastor other than the one they have.

One can tell that the *Discipline's* opening paragraph on appointment making (¶430) was written by clergy; in four long sentences, only one even mentions congregations. The responsibilities of appointment making in the *Discipline*—open itinerancy, physical challenges—while noble, are purely clerical concerns. We found it important for the Cabinet to keep focused on the congregation and its mission. Lay leadership was brought into the process of discernment and asked clearly to define the congregation's mission leadership needs. Lay leadership was often asked for suggestions for pastors who might fill their needs. When appointment making is exclusively the prerogative of the bishop and Cabinet, we rob lay leadership of their power to accept responsibility for decisions about pastors and to help make appointments work. For our system of sending to function well, laity must have faith that the missional needs of the congregation mean more than the care, feeding, and reward of clergy. When Easum and Bandy studied our annual conference (the year before I arrived), they cited the perceived "protection of clergy" as a detriment to our future. A skillful DS provides essential pressure upon a congregation, helps it face the facts of its life together, and raises the level of expectation. Expectation is a great challenge in a declining church. Congregational contentment is a fierce competitor with faithful mission. As I look back upon my appointments of pastors, I have few regrets for the pastors I moved but a number of deep regrets about the pastors I allowed to stay too long in one place.

The system is generally weighted in favor of long pastorates: congregations tend to be content with the status quo. DSs rarely look for more work. If a pastor is not terribly discontent and doesn't want to disrupt his or her family, it is too tempting to leave things as they are. Then comes the DS asking questions like, "Are you pleased with your faithfulness to the mission of Christ?" Focusing congregational leaders' attention upon the numbers, pointing to trends in congregational life, giving the congregation comparative information, sharing stories of how similar congregations in our conference found new life, a wise DS uses a number of stratagems for coaxing a congregation off dead center. Indeed, a questioning, full-of-facts-and-figures DS is one of the greatest gifts our system offers the content-to-the-point-of-moribund congregations.[5]

The process of discussing the possibility of a pastoral transition is known as "consultation" (¶430–¶435 in the *Discipline*). "Consultation" doesn't mean much more in the *Discipline* than "have a conversation about an appointment." We attempted to make consultation mean multiple opportunities for conversation, on a variety of occasions, driven by the facts of a pastor's productivity. In spite of our efforts, one of our pastors asked the Judicial Council for a judgment against me on the basis that he wasn't sufficiently consulted. The Judicial Council ruled one more time that consultation doesn't mean that a pastor is pleased with an appointment, merely that the pastor has been consulted.

Pastors may complain, may bear animosity toward the bishop, and congregations may refuse warmly to welcome a new pastor, but no one can undo the appointive will of a bishop. I pray that the appointive authority of bishops is authoritarianism to a good end. From what I experienced, the authority of bishops to appoint pastors is rarely abused and too modestly used. I was constrained, not by the strictures in the *Discipline,* but rather by my own lack of courage, creativity, and my innate clerical desire to please.

In the North Alabama Conference, once the Cabinet and I determined that a pastor may move, the next step was for the pastor to submit to the DS and to me a DVD of a sermon preached in an actual service of worship. We each responded to the pastor in letters, giving our reactions to the sermon. (It has always seemed odd to the laity that bishops appoint pastors without having heard a pastor preach. I vowed to change that, though as I listened to sixty or seventy sermons during January, I came to regret my vow.)

Then the pastor met with a triad interview team consisting of three members of the Cabinet. These triads proved to be one of our most effective North Alabama contributions to the appointive process. Usually, the pastor was asked to respond in writing to a brief series of questions about his or her ministry and his or her congregation. We tried to keep the questions action oriented: "What has been your greatest success in the past year? What was one thing you did to lead this success?" And, "What was your greatest obstacle to success? What specific steps did you take to overcome that obstacle?" A pastor's spouse was welcomed to the triad consultation. It helped for the spouse, who may be asked to make great sacrifices in an upcoming move, to know that the process is thorough, fair, and prayerfully driven.

Through the triads, each pastor had at least three members of the Cabinet who had spent time understanding the dynamics related to the anticipated move—both to provide the best opportunity for the pastor to utilize his or her strengths in a new appointment and also to understand the needs of the congregation. When the actual decision was made to move a pastor, the triad process insured that we had a variety of insights at the table.

Before our invention of the triad interviews, pastors sometimes said, "My DS doesn't like me," or "My DS doesn't really know me." I never again heard that complaint after the triads. The triads were a major means of making the Cabinet more than a collection of different DSs in eight competing districts. They became a team who worked together with pastors and churches throughout the conference to deploy our best talent where they could get the best results. My first impression of the appointive process was that it was far too focused on the pastor and the pastor's personal and family needs.

"Who is Joe Smith?" I would ask the Cabinet.

Then I was told about Joe's troubled marriage, his wife's emotional difficulties, rebellious children, and his preference "to live somewhere close to Huntsville."

"What does Joe do for a living?" I asked in jest.

"He's a Methodist preacher, of course," they replied.

"I couldn't have surmised that from the information you gave me. What does Joe know how to do for the advancement of the Kingdom of God?"

Cabinet clarity about our obligation to obtain leadership for the church's mission is crucial at every step in the process. Our job, thank goodness, is not to make the pastors' marriages turn out right, or to force their children to behave, or even to help them find happiness and contentment in ministry.[6] We must believe that all these worthy concerns are fruit of a life that is lived in service to the mission of Christ.

Keeping a congregation comfortable is not part of the mission of Jesus Christ. If contentment is the extent of congregational expectation, then we must not to send a pastor who has mission leadership ability.

When I asked a young pastor what was the most important gift I could give him as his bishop, he replied, "Please don't ask me to make dumb, trivial sacrifices for churches that have withdrawn from the mission of Jesus Christ."

Our *Discipline* requires bishops to appoint every elder in good standing (the nefarious so-called guaranteed appointment) without requiring us carefully to evaluate each elder's effectiveness. The number of congregations that can provide an elder's salary and benefits are rapidly shrinking, so the appointive task can be daunting. The minimum financial obligation for having a full-time pastoral position filled by an elder/deacon or a probationary elder/deacon in our conference is over $70,000, including salary and benefits, to say nothing of housing. Lovett Weems of Wesley Theological Seminary showed our Cabinet that a church must average 125 adults in worship to sustain a full-time pastor's salary, an adequate program for growth, an appropriate mission program, maintenance of its facility, and full participation in connectional giving (apportionments). Weems's judgment was a jolt: 60 percent of our elders serve appointments with less than 125 in attendance. The future of Methodism means that more churches will move from full-time to part-time pastors along with a recovery of the historic Methodist practice of churches placed on multiple congregation circuits. Sadly, multiple charge circuits rarely strengthen individual congregations and typify a system in which too many decisions are made for no other purpose than to provide a salary for clergy.

I inherited a schedule whereby the Cabinet arrived at the beginning of the appointive process armed with voluminous files filled with facts and figures on every pastor and church. Overwhelmed by too much data, we lapsed into general impressions and intuition. We now work online with one page of information on each pastor and each church. The pastor's sheet includes: pastor's name, clergy status, marital status, extenuating circumstances, Strengths Finder top five strengths,[7] NCD scores for the church the pastor has recently served, including a seven-year summary of that church's Dashboard benchmarks during the pastor's tenure.

We also take into consideration a pastor's record of leadership in shared missional giving (apportionments). We know which pastors have gifts for leading churches in that uniquely Wesleyan concept of shared ministry, and it is our duty to act on this knowledge. Studies show that if a pastor leads in connectional giving at one church, that pastor will improve the level of giving when appointed to a church that has a poor record of connectional giving. Likewise, a pastor who serves a church that pays only 80 percent of its fair share of apportionments, if moved to a church that pays 100 percent, will lead that church downward.

The key factor in congregational vitality is a pastor's leadership, an intimidating insight for a bishop. Our well-wrought procedures and careful processes, in themselves, do not guarantee a fruitful fit between pastor and congregation. Prudence and prayer are still required. Forgiveness too.

Most leadership books, even those written for clergy, tend to major in practical advice and technique, what Aristotle called "knack," *techne*. In a way, this is as it should be: a widespread clergy skill deficit is experience evaluating systems and then doing what needs to be done to fix things. And yet, as important as knowing how to impact an atrophied church may be, a much greater need for bishops, and much more difficult to attain, is Aristotle's *prudentia*, prudence—applied wisdom.

Good judgment (*phronesis* in Aristotle), the ability to make well-informed, critical decisions, is so important for bishops because (1) few of us clergy have experience making tough decisions and bringing critical judgment to bear upon other people, and (2) in The United Methodist Church, if bishops and DSs don't make well-informed, critical judgments about pastors and churches, *nobody* does.

Good judgments about pastors and churches is a capacity, a set of skills, a habit of character that involves an ability of a leader to obtain accurate and honest information about persons and situations, a capacious appreciation of the complexity and diversity within situations, foresight, a good sense of timing, choice of key subordinates and the knowledge of when to listen to them and when to overrule them, and a mix of humility in the face of the complexities of reality bolstered by a willingness to decide even before facts and outcomes are fully known.[8]

My greatest leadership deficiency: the guts to lead as if Jesus Christ really is Lord.

GETTING OFF TO A GOOD START

One of the Cabinet's most helpful innovations is our First Ninety Days process.[9] Early in my time as bishop, knowing that the first year is a crucial time in the life of a newly appointed pastor, I interviewed recently moved pastors. I was struck by a common theme: pastors who had planned to succeed in their new appointment succeeded. When asked by a congregation, "Why have you been sent to us as our pastor?" those pastors who responded, "Because the Bishop sent me here," usually failed.

I noted that all of our clergywomen, at least all who succeeded, had a strategy for overcoming expected congregational resistance. Savvy clergywomen were unsurprised that they must neutralize opposition and enlist support in order to lead. This led us to require that all pastors who are moving attend First 90 Days Training to help prepare for the transition and to develop a plan for succeeding in their new appointment. Lay leaders in churches that are receiving pastors are also invited to attend an event called "Getting Off to a Good Start: The First 90 Days for Local Church Leaders." This training is designed to facilitate dialogue and partnership between the new pastor and the receiving church. Pastors devise a written plan to share with their DS, who reviews it and then monitors the implementation of the First 90 Days Plan. The plan is shared with the leadership in the local church through a series of conversations held over the initial 90 day period.

We have never had a pastor or church faithfully follow the First 90 Days Plan and have so great a difficulty in the first year that a move was necessary after the first year. Conversely, the abandonment of the plan usually signals that a pastor is not going to succeed in a congregation. Monitoring of the First 90 Days Plan has enabled us to be more timely and responsive to a "bad marriage" between a pastor and congregation, and has resulted in our moving that pastor sooner rather than later.

Every full-time pastor who is moved receives a letter from me and the DS citing specific expectations for results of ministry in the first year: specific, measurable expectations such as "a 10-percent increase in Sunday attendance," or "a 2-percent increase in baptisms of those under 21," or "a 5-percent growth in children's ministry." These letters—signed by me, the receiving DS, the pastor, and key lay leadership—give newly appointed pastors and congregational leadership the tools they need to lead their congregations to grow. A public declaration of the specific expectations that a bishop and Cabinet have in making an appointment give transformative leaders just what they need to hit the ground running.

During their first year in a new appointment all full-time pastors are members of a transition team (newly moved pastors and their DS) that meets regularly and gives them an opportunity to share the skills needed to make the most of the crucial first year.

Our Office of Pastoral Care and Counseling assists pastors and their families who are in stress owing to a move. For every clergy family in stress because of a pastor's commitment to serve where sent, there are dozens more families that know the joy and the satisfaction of being part of a project—the mission of Christ and his church—that is of greater significance even than the individual family.[10]

I am shaken by the knowledge that Italian researchers at the University of Catania, using the Peter Principle (named for Canadian Laurence J. Peter who contended that "in a hierarchy, employees rise to their level of incompetence") tested the theory that competent individuals will be promoted until they reach a job that they cannot perform well, at which point their climb up the corporate ladder ceases and their productivity plummets. Using mathematical modeling, the researchers concluded that promoting top employees will result in a 10-percent drop in efficiency, while randomly advancing your worst employees will result in a 12-percent improvement![11]

Our United Methodist Church is a hierarchy in which great effort is expended advancing our "top clergy" to our "best churches." Would we do as well with a random appointment system in which I gathered with my Cabinet, darts in hand, and tossed the darts at a map of the conference? It's too painful to consider.

The United Methodist practice of itinerancy is so deeply countercultural that we may be unable to sustain it into the future. As I've said, UM polity is against just about everything Americans believe, which has to be one of the reasons early Methodists put so much stress on education and formation—they knew that their version of church required constant indoctrination. And yet John Wigger[12] has taught me that Francis Asbury's great contribution to the formation of Methodism in America was his ability not simply to organize hundreds of Methodist societies in this new land but to teach and to persuade thousands of American Christians that polity, specifically Episcopal Methodist polity, was a gift of God to the mission of the church.

Asbury convinced a Republican culture that the most effective polity was for these powerful superintendents to send (usually) unmarried itinerants to a place where they were needed to accomplish the mission of the church—a decidedly countercultural practice when compared with those church families that relied on married men who were located where they chose to be. The mission of the church is more important than the church's clergy.

So called "guaranteed appointment" in which every elder must receive an appointment every year, regardless of the quality of that elder's work, is indefensible. This provision of the *Discipline* is not only a relic of a time when Methodism lapsed into a sort of club for the benefit of clergy but is also an indicator of lack of trust in bishops. Any time a bishop stiff-arms a congregation into taking a pastor purely because the bishop must have a position for that pastor, when we guarantee every elder an appointment with no structures in place for ongoing evaluation of our elders' work, the guarantee of an appointment becomes an insidious practice that protects and empowers incompetence among a few of our clergy and demoralizes all.

EXITING PASTORS

In a church where clergy watch over clergy we harm the faith the laity place in us if we appear unable to deal with our (fortunately) few inept pastors. We must show that pastors who no longer have the ability to lead a vital congregation are exited from leadership in our church. An increasing number of bishops agree: when bishop and Cabinet cowardly abuse the appointive process to protect the incompetent rather than to remove the inept, the whole UMC suffers.

During my episcopacy, the Cabinet and I, in consultation with the BOOM, exited over thirty pastors who had records of poor performance, a few of whom even had integrity issues that had been overlooked in the past. Multiple, short-term appointments are a sure signal that a pastor is a poor performer. Nearly all exited after frank discussions about their records, though some left under threat that I would draw up an official complaint against them for ineffectiveness. "Here are the facts about your ministry," we told them, "and we are not suppressing the facts from our churches." They withdrew.

I told a few of these pastors, "We now know, based upon painful experience in a succession of congregations, that no UM congregation wants you as pastor. We will not force another congregation to receive you. If resisted, I told some of them, "I hereby give you permission to approach any church in our conference to ask if it is willing to have you as a pastor." All withdrew.

Some bishops are experimenting with various forms of "buy-out" of ineffective pastors, providing funds to exit them as compassionately as possible. That's laudable, if the bishop believes that paying inept clergy to leave is a valid use of the church's resources. I believe that an expensive exit is not necessary for a person who has already taken advantage of the church's graciousness by underserving our people for years.

While I occasionally threatened an unproductive pastor with a formal complaint of ineffectiveness, I was never forced to do this; all of the pastors left voluntarily after some compassionate but direct and skilled conversations by the DSs. The key to effective response to pastoral incompetence is for bishop and Cabinet to keep before us the point of our ministry—to secure the very best pastoral leadership for each congregation. Period. United Methodists place great trust in bishops to oversee the creation, evaluation, accountability, and appointment of our pastors. It is vitally important to the future of our connection that we show we are worthy of their trust.

CHAPTER FOUR

BISHOPS CULTIVATING FRUITFULNESS

The sending of pastors must be built on a bishop's knowledge of the fruits of the pastor's ministry. Jesus loves us enough not only to tell us the truth and to die for our sin but also to hold us accountable for our fidelity. Wesley gave substance to love of God by stressing obedience to God. Any pastor who fails to hold her people accountable for their response to the gospel is not fully practicing the gospel as a Wesleyan. A bishop who refuses to shoulder the responsibility of oversight for assessment and accountability is failing at *episcope*.[1]

In my former life as a college chaplain, the students and I were studying one of Jesus' many parables of judgment. The landowner returns like a thief in the night. Judgment time—reckoning, truth-telling about results, and numerical assessment of fidelity. The students agreed that it is intimidating to know that God promises to hold us accountable for the use of gifts God has given. Then I asked, "Is judgment good news or bad?"

A student blurted out, "Good news!"

Why?

"Because it says that God wants us to succeed at discipleship. God wouldn't command us to take up the cross and follow if God didn't think we could. God cares enough about us to know what we're up to. That's cool."

On his way to the cross, Jesus pauses to curse a fig tree (Mark 11:12-14). Walking past a fig tree in leaf, he notes that the tree bears no fruit. Mark comments that "It was not the season for figs." Refusing to let the season of the year deter him from a negative evaluation, Jesus curses the tree.

Why curse a tree for having no figs when Mark clearly says, "It was not the season for fruit"?

The United Methodist Church has had trouble with fruit for five decades, losing nearly three million members—nearly ten thousand congregations. "The people have moved away," we say. "At least all the people who look like us." Figs have long been out of season.

"Presbyterians and Episcopalians are dying too" is a chief consolation.

The median age of our membership is fifty-nine years old. We have virtually excluded three generations. Young adults are tough to reach—kids have so many more interesting things to do. Over half of our churches have not made a new disciple in the past two years.

"I see no children in your worship," I comment after a Sunday visit.

"We've raised our children and aren't looking to raise anyone else's kids." Our fruitful season is past.

The next day, Jesus and his disciples walked by the fig tree that the day before Jesus had cursed—even though it was not the season for fruit—and yesterday's healthy tree is today withered. If you're a fig tree, better watch your fruit, because if you are unfruitful (in spite of the season of the year) Jesus will curse you to death.

In my conference, about twenty churches a year close. Neither my Cabinet nor I close a church; we are morticians, not murderers. These churches died because fruitlessness in churches is terminal.

A DS told me about a church that was, like most United Methodist churches, comprised mostly of older folk. One of the members' granddaughter brought a friend with her to church. The friend was of a different race than everybody else in the congregation.

The next week the grandmother received a call from one of the church members. "I hope that your granddaughter is not planning to bring her little friend back with her next Sunday. It's not that I am prejudiced, it's just that I am sure the little girl would be happier elsewhere."

The little girl never again visited the church, nor did the grandmother or her granddaughter. They got the message; it's not the season for harvesting fruit.

Less than one year after this event, the DS had the melancholy task at annual conference of reading out that church's name to be closed. "Jesus is just not nice to a church that refuses to be his church," she said.

But it is not the season for figs! We must care for all these older people. And isn't that the purpose of the church and its ministry— to care for our members and their needs?

No fig tree is planted for shade. "You will know them by their fruits" (Matt. 7:16). Somewhere along the line the tree stopped being productive and Jesus, unmoved by naturalistic explanations, curses the fig tree.

Thus church growth guru Bill Easum chided me for speaking of our hundreds of "unproductive churches."

"Don't call them 'unproductive,'" said Easum. "They are 'unfaithful.' Read Matthew 25, then read Matthew 28."

Easum told me when he served as one of my early "outside agitators", "As bishop, your main job is to bless. You will be called on to bless parsonages and new church buildings and to lay your hands on their heads when you ordain them."

Then Easum said ominously, "Be very careful what you bless. God forgive you if you bless infidelity."

Jesus walks by a fig tree in full leaf. He notices no figs, and though it is not the season for figs, Jesus curses the tree. Next day, as Jesus and his disciples walk past the dead tree, Jesus urges his disciples, "Have faith in God," explicitly relating fruitfulness to faithfulness.

Lack we the faith that Jesus can make us fruitful?

THE PERIL OF GOOD NEWS

It is tough to get out good news in our church. One of our congregations grows by leaps and bounds. If I note that this church, unlike most, is growing, there is always some depressed clergyperson nearby to say, "Well, that church is only growing because it happens to be in a good location." Or, "That church is growing because its pastor has made it into a personality cult." Or, "Just good luck." In a declining organization many have a stake in transforming good news to bad, reminding us that we are trapped in a natural, sociologically determined season of decline.

"Everybody else is dying" may be sinful self-consolation due to lack of faith. We have convinced ourselves that, counter to biblical testimony, God is a God of the dead and not the living. Our God may be good but not good enough to surprise us. Death and decline are less threatening to mediocrity than life. Naturalistic, sociological determinism has stunted our once faith-enriched imaginations.

Jesus urges his disciples to "have faith." Do we have faith that God really intends to grow the Kingdom of God? Do we have faith that Jesus Christ is Lord, even master over death and decline, faith that the gospel is able to leap all boundaries and overcome all obstacles?

A suburban pastor told me the main reason it was tough to have a thriving youth group: "Parents would rather their children win in Sunday-morning soccer than succeed in being disciples."

The pastor continued, "But we have *faith* that we can beat them at their own game. We are working with a couple of other churches to form a youth soccer league that doesn't play on Sundays. Our aim is to make it the best league in town."

Now there's a pastor unwilling to submit to the faith of the dominant social order. A productive, fruitful church begins in faith that God really intends for the church to be fruitful and faithful.

Our new campus minister at the University of Alabama, embarrassed that we had reached less than 1 percent of UA students, planned a summer of free concerts and backyard parties in order to "out rush the frats." He told me, "If we don't get a hundred new students in my first year, fire me," warming the heart of this campus minister turned bishop.

Has the season ever been propitious for preaching God on a cross? The same God who bodily raised dead Jesus (sorry, Bishop Sprague[2]) can raise the church, even though fruit is out of season. So Paul admonished young Timothy to "preach the gospel, in season or out" (2 Tim. 4:2 author paraphrase).

I commemorated two hundred years of Methodism in Alabama by reading our history. The Revered Matthew Sturdivant spent a year among our ancestors and pronounced them the "ignorantest race" as explanation for why he was unable to begin any new congregations among the raw Alabamians. At annual conference in Charleston, Bishop Asbury chastised him and sent the hapless Sturdivant back for another year, telling him he would watch his numbers; he had better bear fruit. Thus was Methodism birthed even in the wilds of Alabama.

FRUITFUL FIDELITY

Bishops are discussed in ¶403 of the *Discipline*. These five hundred-plus words on the role of bishops are a nonselective shopping list of all desirable episcopal activities with no attempt to prioritize the absolutely essential. The *Discipline's* ideal bishop has: "a disciplined life . . . a vital and renewing spirit . . . an enquiring mind," and is busy "discerning, inspiring, strategizing, equipping, implementing, and evaluating" along with having "a prophetic voice for justice in a suffering and conflicted world" and "passion for the unity of the church." Oh yes, the bishop must also find time to be "consecrating, ordaining, commissioning, supervising and appointing persons in ministry to the Church and the world."

Of course, no one seriously expects this of a bishop. The cynic in me suspects that the purpose of such a luxuriantly unfocused job description is to rob a bishop of any sense of purpose or agency. So a bishop must find a way to teach the church what bishops are for. Fortunately, we United Methodists have a better theology of the episcopacy in actual practice than is found in the *Discipline*. Mark 11:12-14 suggests that Job One is to pay attention to fruit.

Accountability is resisted by a few of our clergy, not because they are irresponsible, but because the truth hurts. (When you lose over 20 percent of your membership, you don't enjoy talking about it.) Our decline began with our 1968 union, when hubris got the best of us. Being the biggest, we were deluded into thinking that we didn't have to worry about fruit. We focused exclusively on issues of representation, developing a complex system of quotas.[3] The theory behind our polity ceased to be dependence on the Holy Spirit linked with good old Wesleyan productive pragmatism and instead became the assumption that the more people you legislate to be at the table and the more belabored and protracted the discussion, the more faithful.[4]

It has taken us a long time to admit it didn't work, partly because those who set up a system benefit from working the system.

The week after my election, I asked my Duke management coach (who is Jewish) to coach me into my new job. After reading through the *Discipline's* paragraphs on the episcopacy, he said, "Will, as a management consultant, two things bother me about your new job. Not only is there a seemingly intentional vagueness about what your church expects from bishops, but also you are totally unaccountable to anyone. You are as protected as a federal judge!"

By giving bishops much freedom and little accountability, the *Discipline* offers us a God-given opportunity. "Vague expectations leave me free to form the job as I see fit," I said. "I want to be a bishop who makes at least one or two decisions that are so courageous, so maddening to the keepers of the status quo, that someone will say, 'Bishop, thank the Lord that the *Discipline* won't allow us to fire you or you would be history.'"

WATCHING OVER ONE ANOTHER IN LOVE

Still, bishops' lack of accountability for fruitfulness is a detriment to our leadership. One reason the pastoral letters of the Council of Bishops are greeted with a yawn is that the church knows that these public statements cost bishops nothing. When one of my pastors steps up and speaks against unjust Bush/Obama wars without end, that's courageous. When unaccountable bishops speak out, who cares?

Methodism, in the face of Lutheran and Calvinistic suspicions of Wesleyan "works righteousness," maintained, with the Letter of James (beloved by John Wesley to the same degree as Luther despised it), that "faith without works is dead" (James 2:20 KJV). If there's faith, there's fruit. A faithful church is a visible participant in Jesus' move on the world.

We sanctificationists believe in actual "growth in grace," but we have never been so naive as to think that there can be growth without accountability for growth. Wesley's peculiar genius was to devise a network of small groups to be "a company of people having the form and seeking the power of godliness, united in order to pray together to receive the word of exhortation, *and to watch over one another in love that they may help each other to work out their salvation.*"[5]

The phrase "Christian conferencing" is back in vogue among us, but rarely as Wesley used the phrase. For Wesley, "holy conversation" was not an occasion for us to have a civil conversation with one another but rather a providential time for brutally honest, no-holds-barred accountability to one another, a time for mutual confession and forgiveness. Wesley thus made every member of his societies into overseers.

Bishops are virtually unaccountable clergy who have, as a major task, to hold fellow clergy rigorously accountable. Methodism, like Roman Catholicism, is a hierarchical ecclesiastical system in which (unlike much of Catholicism, apparently) clergy are expected to care for and to hold accountable other clergy. This makes all the more odd that though clergy effectiveness is much discussed among us, there is always someone who predictably asks, "What is 'effectiveness' when applied to ministry?"

The purpose of the question is to delay accountability for effectiveness.

In North Alabama we define clergy effectiveness in one biblically based word: *growth*. Effective pastors know how to lead growth. Lists of nice-to-have qualities (¶304 of the *Discipline*) are useless and therefore un-Wesleyan. A pastor who grows things is effective; a pastor who knows only how to lead shrinkage is ineffective.

In counterculturally, belligerently defining effectiveness as growth of the kingdom, the North Alabama Conference restores a Wesleyan agenda to our life together. Early Wesleyans had a passion for reaching the poor and marginalized—not just to perform important social services in their behalf—but rather to welcome the poor into our fellowship and at our table, to witness to the transforming power of God's grace. Growth.

Our elitist, rigorous view of church membership in our early days was combined with an expansive notion of salvation in Jesus

Christ: Jesus Christ atones for the sins of the world, and the whole world is graciously invited to take up the disciplines that lead toward entire sanctification. In any way to limit the scope of Christ's atoning work by restricting the range of our evangelistic invitation and our sanctificationist indoctrination is, for Wesleyans, a sacrilege.

Growth as indicator of clergy effectiveness is abrasive against the status quo; most of the churches served by our pastors will be smaller when the pastors leave than when they arrived. Our seminaries continue to produce pastors who are comfortable serving only one age group (people my age) and those in one socioeconomic level (people with my education and income). "My seminary education," one pastor confessed, "gave me complex rationalization for leading decline and called what it gave me, 'theology.'" Few of our pastors seem to know how to handle a congregation of more than 150 in attendance, shrinking a congregation to a size that is less demanding on pastoral leadership skills.

Though a pacifist at heart, Father John would smack us.

ACCOUNTABILITY

Our Cabinet utilized a helpful book, Lencioni's *Three Signs of a Miserable Job.*[6] What makes a job miserable? *Lack of measurability. Lack of accountability. Anonymity.* When you don't count what you're doing, you don't know what you are doing. When a boss doesn't respect someone enough to count what he or she does, that person is set up for misery.

Lencioni says that "if a person has no way of knowing if they're doing a good job, even if they're doing something they love, they get frustrated."[7] No pastor excels in every area of ministry. "Are all apostles? are all prophets? are all teachers? . . . But covet earnestly the best gifts" (1 Cor. 12:29, 31 KJV). We must help pastors measure and take satisfaction in those areas that are important for the life of the church and demonstrate the gifts that God has given the pastor.

Immeasurement robs pastors of the joy of saying, "God did that through me," or, "I am going to improve in this area and measurement will confirm when I improve." According to Lencioni, "People who aren't good at their jobs don't want to be measured, because then they have to be accountable for something. Great employees love that kind of accountability. They crave it. Poor ones run away from it."[8]

One of my frustrations was that although counting the fruits of our ministry has been at the heart of the Wesleyan movement from the beginning, and although we have a vast, rather expensive system for collecting numbers, as a church we make no decisions on the basis of the numbers. I have dozed through eight hours of numbers from our Board of Pensions, data indicating that our Pension Fund is headed for a disaster. Hey, Board of Pensions, we don't need more numbers; we need decision and action, courage and creativity in response to the numbers.

Bishop Janice Huie taught me that it is a bishop's responsibility to know the fruits of a church's and a pastor's ministry and to administer the appointive process on the basis of that knowledge.

Early on I was asked, "Unlike the last bishop, can we count on you to appoint more women pastors to large churches?"

"I'm not to appoint pastors on the basis of their gender, race, age, seniority, or any criterion other than, 'What does God do through this pastor's ministry?'" I responded. Results. Fortunately, women pastors have amply demonstrated their ability to lead fruitful churches. Sexism is not the chief culprit in our failure fully to utilize our women pastors; it's the seniority system combined with inattentiveness to results. The system of appointing pastors on the basis of seniority, though practiced in every part of our church, is nowhere supported by the *Discipline*. God-given talent is more important than a pastor's years of experience, and God has graciously seen fit to give as many women, many of whom are new to ministry, as many gifts as men for growing a church. What's lacking are overseers of the church with the dogged determination to recognize and then to affirm the gifts that God gives.

Of crucial importance is the need for a bishop and a Cabinet to be clear about their chief purpose, their one great desire: *to appoint the very best pastoral leadership to fulfill the mission of each congregation.* Concerns about an individual pastor's career advancement, familial and marital happiness, gender, ethnic heritage, age, and educational background must be subordinate to the responsibility to appoint the very best pastoral leadership for each church and to encourage every church to demand a pastor who knows how to give that congregation a future.

Of course, all sorts of concerns can be considered in appointing "the very best pastoral leadership for each church." But all are subservient to the one great leadership concern: to serve the mission Jesus gives to a congregation. This is not as tough a job as one might think. We have hundreds of congregations, thousands, without any discernable mission other than the care and comfort of their members. That we have many pastors who have little ability or desire to do much more than care and comfort means that bishops and Cabinets need not struggle to come up with a perfect match. Unfortunately, congregations that exist for no other purpose than care and comfort of their members tend not to be able to pay an adequate salary for an elder.

Recently the *Birmingham News* reported on a number of pastors—all of them under thirty-five, whom I had appointed to some rather large, established congregations. I was praised for my determination to appoint younger clergy to larger churches. While I didn't mind the plaudits, I did want to correct the article. I'm not trying to appoint younger clergy to large churches; I'm trying to appoint effective clergy where they can give congregations a future.[9]

COUNTING AND ACCOUNTABILITY AS WESLEYAN VIRTUES

It is unfair to ask a pastor who has demonstrated an ability only to shrink and retreat the kingdom of God to be an agent of growth. Trouble is, a bishop is overwhelmed by too many numbers, most of which are irrelevant and too old (our published numbers are always two years old).[10]

In North Alabama we created a conference "Dashboard." Every Monday every church logs in (we average 95 percent weekly participation in the Dashboard) and testifies to their numbers for that past Sunday: attendance, baptisms, membership, professions of faith, offering, and hands-on participation in mission. Anyone can see the key indicators for any church in our conference for the past week and over the past three years. All of these numbers have always been reported by every church and pastor throughout the history of Methodism. All we did was to bring the numbers to real time, to limit the number of factors that we measured, and to make the results public.

The push back that we received in this endeavor is what one would expect in a system that has functioned for a long time without attentiveness to results and fruitfulness. I have never had criticism of the Dashboard from a layperson. Nor have we received criticism from clergy who are succeeding. The criticisms were boringly repetitious: "It's all about numbers, is it?" "You can't measure clergy effectiveness, can you?" "So it's come to this: putting the butts in the pews."

There may be something to be said for these slogans—but not in The United Methodist Church. We're Wesleyans. On the basis of Jesus' teaching, we believe in the miraculous growth of the kingdom of God. We must never (as we accused early Calvinists) put limits on the ability of Jesus Christ to save the world. John Wesley had friction with the established church of his day not only because of his vibrant trinitarian theology but also because of his refusal to limit his ministry to the moribund English parochial system and to overlook souls who were being ignored by the church. From the beginning, Methodists were inveterate counters and numbers keepers because, at least until the past forty years, Methodists held themselves accountable to God through numbers.[11]

Richard Heitzenrater discovered something remarkable in the annual minutes of eighteenth-century British Methodism. Beginning in 1769, circuits that had fewer members than the previous year were marked with an asterisk (12 of the 48). By 1779, that number had expanded to 18. (The question was asked at the 1779 Conference, "How can we account for the *decrease* in so many Circuits this year?" The answer: the numerical decrease was "chiefly to the increase of worldly-mindedness and conformity to the world." In 1779 Wesley knew the reason for our present decline!)

As of 1781, Wesley marked with an asterisk those circuits that had an *increase* in membership, which was the case with 32 of them, or exactly half. This method was used for a few years until the percentage of circuits that experienced increases in membership were 75 percent of the connection. Let Wesley be our model.

One of Wesley's main questions referring to his traveling preachers was, "Do they bear fruit?" Francis Asbury's circuit riders reported their numbers to Asbury every six months, and Asbury routinely removed preachers to whom God had not seen fit to give fruitfulness.

Wesley frequently cites numerical growth as indicative of spiritual vitality. In his sermon "On God's Vineyard," Wesley celebrates that the London Methodist Society grew from 12 to 2,200 in just about 25 years. (Heitzenrater speculates that Wesley was trying to spur them on since their membership had slowed to a gain of only 400 new members in the latest 25 years.)

Wesley sent pastors to those areas where, in his estimate, the most souls were awaiting announcement of salvation. He told his traveling preachers not just that they ought to read, but also quantified their reading: five hours a day. The annual conference was invented, not just as opportunity for worship and fellowship, but for rendering account and confessing numbers.

If same-sex orientation and practice is a terribly serious sin, as our *Discipline* now implies, then the Wesleyan question is: How many same-sex practicing sinners have you reached this year? Do you intend to limit Christ's forgiveness to heterosexual sinners?

If we really want an inclusive church, let's start counting the number of new African American UMs we attract each week.[12] I can tell you which of my pastors has a gift for evangelizing Spanish-speaking persons. Have I acted on that knowledge? When Wesley said "grace," he didn't mean feeling that you are a basically good person after all. He meant growth in grace, growth induced by grace, grace given to bear fruit.

I can't speak for other church families, but in the Wesleyan family, studied obliviousness to results, deployment of pastors without regard to fruitfulness, pastors shrinking churches, pastors keeping house among the older folks left there by the work of a previous generation of conscientious pastors, and churches having a grand old time loving one another and praising God without inviting, seeking, and saving those outside the church do not make for Wesleyan faithfulness.

In Wesley's "Address to the Clergy," in which he outlined his expectations for the performance of his traveling preachers, he stressed *grace*—visible response to God's work in their lives, *gifts*—they must show both God-given talents and skills for ministry, and *fruit*—visible, measurable evidence of God's blessing their ministry.[13] Seen from this perspective, Methodism is a theological movement that defines faith by its fruits and prays for, expects, celebrates, and holds itself accountable to results—and is willing to change anything about itself in order to be more obedient to Christ's mandate.

Mission is what you measure. Numbers don't show everything about the church and its ministry, but they are reliable indicators of spiritual vitality and a major way of focusing and energizing our ministry. One of our slogans in the Cabinet has been, "You only count what's important and *whatever you count becomes important.*"[14]

Christians cannot live without asking the basic, quantifiable question that Jesus asks in a number of his parables: "What have you done with what you have been given?" What most mainline churches have measured, judging from our paltry results, are harmony, stability, and the retention of power by those who are already in the church. When I propose a pastoral move, an all-too-frequent response from the lay leadership is, "Why are you moving our pastor? We love Jim, Jim loves us. We are doing great." It's then (with Janice Huie as my model) that I pull out their woeful statistics and say, "You and Jim have a wonderful time at your love-in because, according to my estimates, in ten years it's over."

Not that we haven't been measuring anything; we've been counting matters that—from a biblical point of view—are unimportant. Show me where Jesus gives a rip about harmony, stability, and the retention of power by those who are here. A mantra that I and my Cabinet repeat when we get resistance concerning our stress on growth is "Jesus Christ loved the world, not just the church" (see John 3:16). When the GCRR tells me that the most important thing I can do as a bishop to have a more inclusive church is to insure that more racial ethnic clergy are elected to our GC delegation, one knows why our proportion of ethnic minorities is shrinking. It's all in what you count.

Negativity about quantification of mission and ministry is a relatively new phenomenon in our church.[15] Critics who charge, "Willimon has capitulated to a capitalist business mentality in his stress on numbers," show their own confinement in a culture that says, "Christians are out-of-date in our brave new secular world and are destined to die. Resurrection is a lie." The church must free itself, not from overdependence on business practices of leadership and management, but rather from capitulation to almighty sociological determinism that says we are fated to irrelevancy in a secular, godless culture. The church becomes revolutionary when it begins to count what it's doing and holds itself accountable to the demands of Jesus.[16]

As American Christians bought into the anti-Christian idea that religion is something that you privately, personally consume, a vague feeling rather than a politically, organizationally embodied movement, we adopted the docetic notion that it was crude to ask, "How many people have you succeeded in getting out of bed and engaging in worship of the Trinity on a Sunday morning?"

I log into the Dashboard every week and note those churches that have experienced the most fruit that week and contact pastors, asking what one thing they have done to produce such great results. I have learned much about leadership from these conversations. The main purpose of the Dashboard is to assist the leadership of the local church, by giving them the tools they need to lead their congregation. When they note factors like average attendance, a rising median age, or shrinking resources for ministry, they are worrying about someone other than themselves. They are doing a very Wesleyan thing: focusing on who is *not* here, worrying about someone in need who is *not* being noticed. Thus we have discovered that, of all the numbers, the "AVM" (Sunday attendance as a percentage of church membership) is by far the most revealing.

It wasn't a bureaucratic bishop who sent out disciples to make more disciples, feed more hungry, heal more sick, cast out more demons, and forgive seventy times seven—it was Jesus! A church all full of platitudes but devoid of much discernable fruit is the sort of church that Jesus warned against, a church that had all the right slogans, like "Lord! Lord!" but failed to combine its declarations of love with actual instances of obedience.

If I called a pastor of any vital church in my conference on Sunday afternoon (as I have often done) and ask, "How did things go today?" the pastor immediately responds with the exact numbers of worshipers, amount of money received for mission and ministry, and the number of baptisms. I rest my case.

I may tell you that I am on a diet, but until I get on the scales and note the numbers, I'm not on a diet.

CALL TO ACTION

A major impediment to my leadership in holding pastors more accountable for their results was that bishops are unaccountable for the fruits of our labors. In discussions of the nefarious, so-called guaranteed appointment for elders, I've had to admit that we bishops are guaranteed an appointment without accountability. Of course, we should remove so-called guaranteed appointment for our clergy. First, let's remove unaccountable, lifetime tenure for bishops. While active, bishops should be placed by the jurisdictional episcopacy committee on the basis of a fair and accurate assessment of our ability to lead growth. Bishops should be retained, moved, or removed by focusing intently on what we most need bishops to do. Until that happens, bishops will be hindered in our ability to oversee our clergy.[17]

It's difficult to force someone to be accountable; accountability must be assumed by people as they answer the question "For what do you personally take responsibility in service to our church?" This is followed by: "How will we know when you have been responsible?" Selective, public, shared quantification is essential to a culture of accountability.

We must not wait for epicopal committees (ECs) to step up and fulfill their responsibilities (I have yet to hear of an EC that functions well) before bishops step up and fulfill ours. The only occasion when a UM pastor is not appointed by a bishop is when bishops are appointed by the jurisdictional episcopal committee. The EC could learn a thing or two about skilled appointment of bishops from bishops—if they would only ask.

The good news is that bishops are beginning to model accountability. While this book was in its initial stages, the COB unanimously approved the Call to Action report (umc.org/calltoaction). This was a sign of a remarkable shift in attitudes among our bishops. A movement that began with bishops working in their conferences in different ways has fundamentally changed the conversation in the general church with North Alabama leading the way. After decades of denial and obliviousness, the bishops tell the truth of "our increasingly older membership and aging leaders; declines in the numbers of professions of faith, worship attendance, and baptisms; and growing financial burdens accompanied by decreasing revenues."[18]

Then the report states the goal of episcopal leadership at this time and place:

> The adaptive challenge for The United Methodist Church is to redirect the flow of attention, energy, and resources to an intense concentration on fostering and sustaining an increase in the number of vital congregations effective in making disciples of Jesus Christ for the transformation of the world.

The bishops recognize that the Holy Spirit works from the bottom up, from the local church, more than from the general church down.

Noteworthy among the five recommendations was "Measure progress in key performance areas using statistical information to learn and adjust approaches to leadership, policies, and use of human and financial resources" in order that we could lead from "fact-based and not opinion-based" criteria. Lest anyone think that we bishops were dodging accountability for ourselves, CTA said that we would "reform the Council of Bishops, with active bishops assuming responsibility/accountability for improving results in attendance, professions of faith, baptisms, participation in servant/mission ministries, benevolent giving, and lowering the average age of church participants, as well as for establishing a new culture of accountability throughout the church."[19]

On the day that the CTA was released, a professor of theology wrote to tell me that she was in tears over our Dashboard and accused me of betraying my *Resident Aliens* principles, putting "numbers before people." This is code for "stop putting us in pain" and "who are you to hold us accountable?"[20]

I told this professor that if I had my druthers I would have had us count in the manner of Duke Divinity School: how many

African Americans are enrolled? How many women are we preparing for ministry? I give thanks that Duke, like all of our schools of theology, now pays attention to and makes decisions on the basis of numbers.

Our church puts about sixty times more money into clergy pensions, caring for retired clergy, than it puts into youth ministry. Are you surprised that my church has a median age of fifty-nine? Every year I ordain new clergy who have borrowed to pay their educational costs. (Twenty ordinands entered our annual conference last year with cumulative educational debt of nearly a million dollars.) Clergy educational debt could be the death of the appointive system. My conference provides free retirement housing for our retired elders and, as with all our conferences, provides dangerously underfunded and over-benefited pensions. The way we use our resources is a commentary on our theology, a sign that our past is more valuable to us than our future.

As this book was going to press, Bishop Schol announced that the congregations of the North Alabama Conference were among the most vital in the UMC on the basis of the indicators of vitality as reported in the Vital Congregatons Initiative. Bishop Schol also noted that all of the ten most vital conferences had one thing in common—we all stressed metrics as a means of encouraging vital congregations.

Noticing numbers doesn't change anything; noticing numbers is essential for changing everything. Fortunately, Wesley and Asbury made us Christians who care about numbers because we have a mandate to care about what Christ commands.

I sent a pastor to a declining church in east Alabama, telling her, "You could well be the last to serve this congregation," to which she replied, "not if God answers prayer." Shortly after she arrived there, I saw what she meant. I noticed her numbers gradually moving upward, the first positive movement in a decade in that congregation I called her and asked what she was doing to make a difference.

"I spend an hour a day in prayer, saying, 'Jesus, if you want us to grow, send us some children.' We repainted our dingy, unused children's Sunday school rooms. I got three people to volunteer to be teachers. They asked, 'who are we going to teach?' I told them, 'You show up every Sunday with a prepared lesson and, if no children show up, you are to sit there and pray for God to send us some.' Three weeks later, two little children showed up out of nowhere. So I told the teachers that we needed to double our time in prayer since we were on a roll. Next week, six children showed up. We're up to twenty now and we are not going to stop until it's a hundred. Every one of those children counts in the kingdom."

Like I said, our best pastors long to be held accountable, and in ministry you only count what's important and whatever you count becomes important.

CHAPTER FIVE

BISHOPS LEADING CHANGE

L ong before he was Bishop of Rome, Cardinal Ratzinger gave a lecture extolling the virtues of Holy Mother Church, the Church of Rome. Afterward my favorite theologian, Karl Barth, "humbly" asked, "But how do you know your magnificent church and its glorious practices were not a clever escape from the Holy Spirit?"[1]

It's an honest question for a bishop of any time and place—how does your leadership hinder the Holy Spirit?[2]

Bishop Robert Schnase described the ecclesiastical challenge he inherited:

> I was assigned nine hundred congregations. Under the leadership of faithful bishops, pastors, and laypersons, the conference had lost eighty-five thousand members in forty years, closed two hundred churches, and watched the median age rise to fifty-eight. I saw the profound nature of the crisis, seemingly insurmountable and irreversible . . . These staggering trends marked us as "average" among mainline churches.[3]

Bishop Schnase's despair signals a change in the attitude of our bishops—after decades of denial, bishops are telling the truth. Thus Bishop James Swanson opened his sermon to the newly ordained in my conference with, "I don't know what you have been told, but we are a church in trouble. God has sent you to us and we need your help now!"

Holy Spirit-induced leadership tells the truth and then leads change.

The low ebb in my episcopacy came early. We newly elected bishops—fresh from a grueling election campaign in which we had all attempted to appear not to be campaigning—were subjected to "Orientation." I thought we would be taken to a room and told, "We are in trouble. Here's the ledger. See for yourself. We have been waiting for you to help us get our church in gear. Got any ideas?"

Orientation was none of that. It was, "Here's how we have done things. Watch carefully so you will know how to do things as we have done things so that we are assured that you will continue to do things the way we have always done."

Some of us novice bishops revolted. We assembled resources whereby we could acquire the skills and understandings needed not simply to manage the church as it was but rather to lead the church to what it wanted to be. Contemporary episcopal authority must question past authority if we are to move the church forward.[4]

While it's true that our church began as a confraternity of traveling preachers who set out to renew the church and to spread "scriptural holiness" everywhere, rescuing as many as possible "from the wrath to come," and our polity continues to be one in which clergy watch over clergy, our church is too clerically driven. Though the oversight of clergy is important, every morning a bishop must jump out of bed and say, "I work primarily for Jesus Christ and his church, and only secondarily for the care and feeding of clergy."

Through the ages, the baptized have been all too willing to transfer their baptismal responsibilities onto the backs of clergy. Examples: The General Commission on the Status and Role of Women (COSROW) cares not for the role and status of women but only for clergywomen. Or, our conference treasurer hands the conference budget to me, I pass it to the DSs, who lay it on their clergy, who then "raise apportionments" from the laity. How did the financing of the general church's ministry become the sole responsibility of us clergy? Does the Priesthood of all Believers mean nothing? My dream, quite unrealized, is for us clergy to empower the laity to act in our conference as in every congregation—to take responsibility for the finances of the church.

TAKING RISKS, CHANGING LIVES

Our Constitution says that our church is for "the maintenance of worship, the edification of believers, and the redemption of the world."[5] In our conference we put a sharper point on our purpose, the Vision of the North Alabama Conference: *Every church challenged and equipped to make more disciples for Jesus Christ by taking risks and changing lives.*[6]

Note that our Vision fails even to mention clergy, including bishops. Furthermore, my task has been to challenge and to equip rather than to perform, to execute, or to produce. All I have done (did I say "all"?) is to challenge and equip churches to be prepared to be walloped and commandeered by the Holy Spirit so that they take risks and lead changed lives rather than do what comes naturally.

In 2009, with my encouragement, the conference added one word to the Vision in order to quantify and thus build accountability into our work: *Every church challenged and equipped to make **more** disciples for Jesus Christ by taking risks and changing lives* (Emphasis Jesus Christ's).

My job could be unmanageable were it not for the Vision. When some dear soul makes the hackneyed complaint, "Clergy morale is low in our conference," or asks, "What have you done to end stress among our overburdened pastors?" what joy there has been to shove this sentence before them with, "Sorry. Not my job. Here's what is expected of me (and you). The test of my ministry is how well God uses me to challenge and to equip every church to make *more* disciples for Jesus Christ by taking *more* risks and changing *more* lives."[7]

The Vision helped me decide for what I was most responsible, what is most needed of me at this time and place in our connection, and studiously avoid distractions. Bishops, once so fatigued by much busyness, can teach and lead others now as much by what we fail to do as by what we do.[8]

First month on the job, I asked our director of new church development, "What do you most need from me?"

I thought he would say, "Give me a million dollars to start new churches."

Instead he responded, "A few clergy who are willing to risk."

"It's The UMC!" I said. "We've created an ecclesiastical system whereby clergy are protected from ever having to take any risk whereby they might be hurt by Jesus!"

While recruiting seminarians, one callow youth asked me, "Bishop, if I come to your conference, can I be sure that you will back me up if I have conflict with the laity?"

She must know our bloody history. Summoning more candor than usual, I replied, "I promise never to allow anything worse to happen to you than happened to our Lord. I'm just a bishop, after all. I'm impotent to protect you from the perils of work with Jesus."

Our conference found it necessary to recruit and then to credential clergy from outside The United Methodist Church in order to start new churches. I'm unsure whether The UMC is a haven for risk-averse people or we make people cautious once we ordain them. Odd. Methodism's itinerate, appointive practices are the most demanding and dangerous clergy deployment system in Christendom. And fun too.

In self-examination I admitted that I was spending most of my time engaged in activity that could not be honestly correlated to the Vision. I intentionally set a goal of at least half of my time spent "challenging," and "equipping," by "taking risks and changing lives" and to have the courage to refuse to be drawn into activity that did not contribute to the accomplishment of our mission.[9]

I appointed a woman to lead a church that had languished at the same location for seventy years, stuck in a declining neighborhood. In one year she led them to relocate two miles closer to the highway ("We want you to go with us," she told recalcitrant members, "but we're moving, with you or without you"). Because I have never relocated a church, I stand in awe of her leadership skills. I spent time shadowing this pastor, observing her at work, asking her, "Teach me how you do what you do. I've got a whole conference in need of relocation."

Vision alone is insufficient to propel change; there must be specific, measureable, datable goals that prioritize the work. We asked, "What few things would our conference need to do to make our Vision our reality?" Our Cabinet devised five priorities:

- New Congregations
- Natural Church Development Leading to Healthy Congregations
- Effective Leadership
- Empowering a New Generation
- Missions

My first impulse was to put these priorities to a vote by the conference (how hard it is to break old ways of thinking!). Then we decided that the Cabinet had worked hard to take an honest, informed assessment. It is too much to expect everyone to be on board with priorities before they've experienced them, particularly people who were produced by another vision. Let's simply announce our priorities and watch how the conference reacts. We plastered them on our website and every bit of printed matter, and we conducted our annual charge conferences on the basis of the priorities, asking pastor and congregation, "What have you done this year to participate in each of our priorities?"

Earlier, when a DS annually met with each pastor, the conversations tended to be, "How are you and the family doing?" or "Where do you see yourself in your next appointment?" Now DSs disciplined themselves to keep the conversation focused on the five priorities: "Whom did you last have a hand in calling into the ordained ministry?" and "Tell me what you did to cultivate the most recent person whom you baptized?"

Each year we organized our annual conference around one priority, enabling it to be a time of teaching rather than a time to hear reports and to legislate. One summer, Adam Hamilton equipped us in effective leadership and was followed by guided clergy conversations to share how we were putting Adam's ideas into practice.

Our annual conference no longer has people troop through and read reports, bring greetings, and introduce other distractions. "If your report is focused on the priority under discussion, fine," we told them. "If not, we will print it in the *Journal.*" One of our most memorable presentations was that of Cam West, president of our Huntingdon College, who began his report with, "I am thrilled that you have made 'empowering a new generation' your priority. Let me tell you how Huntington is an essential partner in this work."

How delightful it is to see the Council On Bishops catching the spirit of focus, accountability, and prioritizing that we have pioneered.[10] The Bishops' Call To Action report stresses that we must decide "what is *most* essential to achieve the mission." Focus requires, "a reduction of the number and size of general agencies." By my estimate, over half of all of our general church boards and agencies are not up to the CTA's criterion of "essential to achieve mission." They serve an old vision that the church is called to do a myriad of tasks without taking responsibility for accomplishing the most important, all undergirded by dated notions that nothing good happens except from the top down. The for CTA is right that our boards and agencies must be reconstituted, placing emphasis on results rather than representation, and must "overcome current lack of alignment, diffused and redundant activity, and high expense due to independent structures."

NOT LEAVING WELL ENOUGH ALONE

As United Methodist clergy, bishops are prone toward stability, continuity, systemization, and management more than to transformative leadership. Most of us bishops were elected because we were successful at being clergy who ingratiate ourselves to fellow clergy. The current ecclesiological system produced us, so it is quite a challenge to critique, transform, and renovate the church rather than simply to care for fellow clergy. For most of us bishops, our most daunting transformational challenge is ourselves.

My conference's well-organized response to recent devastating Eastertide tornadoes was a highlight of my episcopacy. Time and again, as Patsy and I visited our damaged churches (we lost twenty) or the dozens of relief centers, we heard, "We are more church than we were before." Dozens of our pastors rediscovered themselves as servant leaders in the aftermath of the storms. Something about Jesus weaves even a storm into his redemptive work.

After the storms I discovered that those who disbelieve in "change for the sake of change" are wrong, particularly in a moribund institution with so many means of self-protection. Sometimes we resemble a closed union shop for the protection of clergy mediocrity. Change, even when we don't know where it is headed, opens space for the Holy Spirit to intrude and show us what God can do.

"How's your new bishop?" one of our pastors was asked by a buddy. He replied, "We've been tsunamied."

My management coach said, "Will is a change magnet—he magnetically attracts people who want change and he repulses people who don't." I therefore: cancelled the bishop's convocation on ministry and led three hundred of our clergy to the Gulf Coast in a week of Katrina recovery work, asked churches to let me lead the Eucharist whenever I visited; cancelled the monthly conference magazine, which had $150,000 in subsidy and only 2,000 subscribers, and moved to web-based communication; chose as my first assistant a young woman just a couple of years out of seminary; reduced our districts from twelve to eight; begged churches to send only their best young leaders to our annual conference; junked our connectional ministries structure and started over, making every job fight for its continuance; collected Alabama visionary folk art for our new United Methodist Center; placed remaining connectional ministries personnel in local churches from whence they conducted their work; reduced our conference budget by 15 percent in order that the conference budget work like local church budgets, with the projected budget aligned to expected income; allowed some districts to permit churches to abandon the apportionment formula and move to a straight tithe of income; refused to attend district meetings for everyone and instead met frequently with selected groups of clergy and laity who had positive impact on our results; and removed the bishop's reserved parking space. I had no idea if any of these changes would be fruitful. It's a blessing to lead an organization that's failing in numerous ways; one can jettison accustomed practices and risk trial and error without fear of messing up a good thing.

Disruption is an essential component of organizational innovation.[11] Failure to allow disruption is leadership arrogance. Many United Methodists voted for me to be a bishop because they craved somebody who would enjoy Jesus' inclination to bring in the kingdom of God through shake, rattle, and roll. Our beloved church is in need of critique and disruption in the service of transformation and renovation—and there is no way to do that without being willing to generate sometimes painful friction. Maybe there was a time when a bishop needed to be a calming, benign presence—the fourth-century in Asia Minor, perhaps. In the present hour, bishops are a gift of God to the church for prodding, disciplining, and threatening reformation.

In Alabama it's grace that a few of our eldest clergy engaged in social activism and various forms of civil disobedience. I treasure a faded copy of "Letter from a Birmingham Jail," mimeographed for "Bombingham" clergy. Martin Luther King, Jr.

justifies why he has organized marches and sit-ins that "disturbed the peace."

> "Why sit-ins, marches and so forth? Isn't negotiation a better path?" You are quite right in calling for negotiation. . . . Nonviolent direct action seeks to create such a crisis and foster such a tension that a community which has constantly refused to negotiate is forced to confront the issue. It seeks so to dramatize the issue that it can no longer be ignored.

King's letter explains that although he opposes *violent* tension, he believes there is "a type of constructive, nonviolent tension which is necessary for growth":[12]

> So must we see the need for nonviolent gadflies to create the kind of tension in society that will help men rise from the dark depths of prejudice and racism to the majestic heights of understanding and brotherhood.

The purpose of protests is "to create a situation so crisis-packed that it will inevitably open the door to negotiation." The liberal recipients of King's letter (one of whom was a Methodist bishop) hoped that Birmingham would desegregate without a fight. King eloquently told them they were wrong.[13]

The peace that King disturbed was no peace, but instead Birmingham's police state, constructed by powerful people in order to oppress and terrorize black citizens. (Racist, virtual city dictator Bull Connor was a Methodist.) No transformation without disruption.

In the Bayeux Tapestry, toward the end of the panorama, a mitered man on a horse menacingly aims his long lance at the rear ends of a squad of soldiers in front of him. The inscription below reads, "Bishop Odo comforts his soldiers."

That's comfort worthy of bishops! I marvel whenever I hear that a congregational church is renewed. How do they change without a bishop relentlessly comforting them forward?

As the *Discipline* says, we are "servant leaders." What does that mean? Someone said, "You are the most doggedly persistent, relentless, and argumentative person I've ever known." Though I took it as high compliment, I'm not ordained to be "persistent" or "relentless;" In the name of Christ I'm ordained to service to the church. Decisiveness fits me no more naturally (I was a university professor for two decades!) than preaching, on a weekly basis, a crucified Savior. Fortunately, our Service of Ordination promises us clergy neither personal fulfillment nor pleasure in the exercise of servanthood.[14] When our *Discipline* calls us "servant leaders," the particular service required of bishops, at this time and place, is conversion, detoxification, and change of the church.

Leadership is needed only if an organization feels called to go somewhere. Specifically Christian leaders are convinced that deep transformation is initiated and driven by God. So one of the challenges of church leadership is to be the sort of leader whom God uses to exhort people to believe that we have a God who is able. One doesn't have to be a Wesleyan Christian to work organizational change but being a Wesleyan-sanctificationist-perfectionist-conversionist really, really helps.[15]

One of my pastors asked, "Bishop, do you really believe our conference will continue the changes you have initiated? I fear we're going to fall back into our old ways when you leave."

"I had a man in my church who was a drunk for thirty years," I responded. "Jesus healed him. Don't tell me Jesus can't make us the church he means for us to be."

God did not create the present structure and rules of The United Methodist Church—we did. Our present way of doing God's business stems from 1964 to 1972 when, in order to unite the Methodist Church to the Evangelical United Brethren, we forced our church into an (already) outdated, corporate-America way of organizing.

I once thought the most difficult task was to formulate a vision. It's not. In an incarnational faith the challenge is to incarnate our commitments. Finding the funding to begin a dozen new churches a year was easy compared with having to learn and to embed procedures for vetting, equipping, and supervising new church pastors. (Most of our training of pastors is, unintentionally, to prepare them to serve shrinking centenarian congregations.)

In Barth's 1934 Barmen Declaration, a segment of the church stood up to Hitler by asserting that we are saved through the preached Word of the church, not by obedience to the state. Barth stated that the church

> has to testify in the midst of a sinful world, with its message as with its order, that it is solely his property, that it lives and wants to live solely from his comfort and his direction.[16]

Barth, who loved the preached word more than the structures of the church, saw internal church order as a witness to the world, a rebuke to Hitler. The church must care for its structures, not because if it doesn't it may die, but because we want to be more faithful to a living, Trinitarian God. Many intelligent, theologically well-formed pastors are unable to incarnate their high principles in a congregation because they arrogantly refuse to grow in their basic management and administrative skills. A church that's full of good intentions and slack on practical witness is a church of docetic admirers rather than incarnated followers of Jesus.

When our clergy elected members of General Conference, despite my urging for young clergy and racial and gender inclusiveness, they elected mostly the same persons they had elected before. Only one of the clergy elected to GC serves a church that participates fully in connectional giving—even though GC approves the general church budget![17]

The vote signaled, "We are threatened by youthful, productive clergy and we are determined to protect the *status quo ante episcopos.*"

My Cabinet had made greater gains in inclusiveness, in recognizing young talent, and in honoring effectiveness by their appointments than had our clergy when voting for the future of the church. While the vote indicated that I had been unsuccessful in winning over the majority of our clergy to a different future, it did show the extraordinary courage of our Cabinet in leading change.[18]

How People Transition through Change

I have been helped by a little book on change, *Managing Transitions: Making the Most of Change* by William Bridges.[19] Bridges distinguished between "change" and "transition." *Change* is situational and external—the growing secularity of Americans, the suspicion that Americans have toward large, historic institutions like denominations, the influx of other cultures into the United States. *Transition* is internal, that which needs to happen within the organization as a result of the change that's going on around it in order for the change to be engaged, orchestrated, and exploited—structural reorganization, a new statement of mission, different personnel who have gifts for transformation. Our church finds itself jerked around by social forces we didn't create. Bridges said that agents of change see external conditions as a call for strategic decisions and actions, a call for leadership. As we move into a time of change, Bridges said that we find ourselves in predictable states:

Endings
Letting go is often accompanied by grief and sometimes relief. Change begins with ending. The major issue in this phase is loss of attachment, influence, power, security, meaning, and relationships. People suffer from the loss of illusions like "If we just stay the course, keep positive, and work harder, we will get different results" or "United Methodism has always been an innovative, liberal, diverse church" or "The thing I used to love about our conference was that I knew everyone and we are all working together." In this phase it is important to honor the past and

acknowledge what has been done up to this point, yet with the understanding that the past must not hold us captive. The most frequent response I heard from hurt, retired clergy or bishops was "You don't appreciate what we've done for the church in the past." In any ending, expect "Why us? Why now? What did we do wrong? Why weren't we told sooner? Is there a hidden agenda?"

Neutral Zone

This is the in-between area of change. Limbo. People feel disoriented, neither here nor there. Lack of clarity fosters anxiety over the future. Bridges said that people are often less productive and less motivated during this phase. Rumors abound. People search for facts, but are distressed when the answers they get from their leaders seem vague. Much energy is expended in what Bridges called "recreational complaining."

"Bishop, are you sure these changes will lead to better results?"

"I only know that if we continue doing what we have always done we will get the same results that we've always gotten," I replied.

Note that Jesus begins his ministry in the wilderness, faced with Satan's challenge to his messianic identity and mission. Tempting alternatives were set before him. He resisted. Thus this limbo time is a time of sorting through what we want to do and what we refuse to keep doing. I feel that all of my episcopacy was spent in a trackless terrain where the way ahead wasn't obvious; a bishop in Bridges's neutral zone.

And yet this can be a very fruitful period. Leaders must resist the temptation to rush through the crisis and devise easy solutions. It's a time of experimentation and breakthrough possibilities for trial-and-error exploration.

I pushed for a shorter, more efficient annual conference, moving from more than four days to fewer than two. "We are losing our community, our connectedness," critics said. "I remember when we looked forward to AC as a time of fellowship." (I had no such complaints from laity.) I suspected that for some clergy, a protracted annual conference provided the illusion that we are actually accomplishing something by enduring a tiresome, week-long meeting. To be fair to critics, we had a clash of purposes. I stressed efficiency and productivity; they valued fellowship and connection. It was important for me to be honest that, while I anticipated some gains, there would also be loss. I also might be wrong.

I confess that I am constitutionally ill-suited to leadership in this neutral zone. I'm impatient. I tire of hearing the same old complaints (don't you love Bridges's "recreational complaining"?). For the people of North Alabama Methodism, an impatient, exasperated, loquacious bishop is the bishop they got.

New Beginnings

At last we reach new rules, new roles, and increasing acceptance and commitment to a new vision. People step up and express a more positive mood, saying, "We knew we needed to change. We just couldn't figure out how." (I heard that in my annual conference after four years of work.) The organization reaps the benefits of improved productivity and increased clarity, but there is lingering fear about being successful in a new environment. After teaching our annual conference, Lovett Weems told me, "I think you are going to do a lot of good and you are doing many of the right things, but I worry that the massive decline is going to make people lose heart before the job is done." New people are called to leadership, people who step up and ask, "How can I contribute?"

Four tasks confront leaders of change, said Bridges. Give people:

Purpose—help people understand the main thing that we're trying to accomplish with the changes.

Picture—help people imagine a different future than the one to which they feared that they were fated.

Plan—outline steps and schedule when people will receive information, evaluation, support, and training.

A **Part to Play**—help people fulfill their new role and relationship to the new world.

And then we start all over again. Bridges said that change tends to come in waves and in any healthy institution (and I would add, in service to any living God), change is constant. There's always something to be fixed, some new task to be assumed. The leader must not attempt to manage all change but interpret, re-assure, and encourage. If our church is to keep up with the movements of the risen Christ, we must all gain more skills in fomenting constant change, in serving Christ at one point in time, and then doing it all over again at another time and place. We've got to be constant in our commitment to our focused purpose, but we must be supple in our strategies. The leader must foster a culture such that when strategic mistakes are made, they are acknowledged, and a new strategy is developed without wasting time feeling guilty that the strategy didn't work.[20] Such are the demands of preserving a vibrant institution and of keeping pace with the machinations of the living Christ.

We are not there, but at least we are on the way, which from the Exodus to the beginning of the way (Acts 2), is the only place the people of God have ever been. Because of the nature of the Trinity, two important theological commitments for any pastor, especially one who would lead change are: (1) A robust, extravagant confidence that the Holy Spirit can keep the church in motion, and (2) A courageous commitment to follow the Holy Spirit in order to bear greater fruit of the Spirit.

GRACE TO CHANGE

Dick Heitzenreiter has noted that Wesley's question of prospective preachers was, "Do they have gifts and grace?" not, as one often hears in our church, "Do they have gifts and grace*s*?"

that is, do they show evidence that the transformative grace of God is working in their life?

In his *Plain Account of Christian Perfection,* Wesley defends taking seriously Jesus' "Be perfect as your heavenly Father is perfect." Conversion, growth in grace, relentless and even ruthless self-criticism (how can there be growth without honesty and repentance?) became a way of life in the Wesleyan Societies. To my mind, one of Wesley's great theological contributions was his reiteration that Jesus—the Word made flesh—is not only God with us but also God working in us. Grace is not a sappy "I love you just as you are; promise me you won't change a thing," divine forbearance of our status quo. Grace is the power of God that miraculously enables us to live better lives than if we had not been given transformative grace. In the episcopacy, I have learned first-hand that Jesus does not command us to do impossible things but enables us to do things that would be impossible without God's grace.

The Exodus out of Egyptian slavery begins with God summoning Moses to leadership (Exod. 3). Moses is an unlikely liberator—a hot-headed, tongue-tied murderer. A bush bursts into flame and a divine voice thunders, "I have seen the captivity of my people and I have come down to deliver them from Pharoah." God has acted to save God's people. How?

"*You* go before Pharoah and *you* tell Pharoah to let my people go."

Moses protests—he is not a gifted preacher, he has no credibility with the powerful. The voice simply orders, "Go!"

This has long been a paradigmatic story of faithful vocation, of an unlikely person selected for a mission. Moses is sent to be a prophet—speaking truth to power—so that God's people can be in motion from slavery to liberation.

The truth that must be spoken to power is often a disrupting, disregarded truth, a truth that dislocates the powerful and puts the prophetic speaker in peril. Bishops, like all preachers, identify with the call of Moses. The powerful to whom we truth-telling contemporary prophets must now speak represent the powerful status quo and its servants. Our church is full of people who think of themselves as theological liberals but who are organizational reactionaries. The power of convention does not give way easily, thus the change-oriented bishop learns to rely on the same power that emboldened Moses, the divine authorization that says not only "Go!" but also "I will be with your mouth and teach you what you are to speak" (Exod. 4:12).

Of this I am a witness.

SELF-DIFFERENTIATED LEADERS

Bishops are the most itinerate of UMC pastors. I wish we could change my designation from "Resident Bishop, Birmingham Area" to something more itinerate like, "Bishop in Motion, Mainly in North Alabama." By serving elsewhere than our home conference, bishops are placed in a unique position to lead. This enables us to cultivate what Rabbi Edwin Friedman called "self-differentiation."[21] A good leader, said Friedman, must be "separate while still remaining connective." It is easier to develop strong personal relationships with people than to "take stands at the risk of displeasing."

Gil Rendle told my Cabinet that they must give me adequate "balcony time." Someone has got to be detached enough to take the long view and assess the overall direction of the church. Critical perspective is aided by distance. A bishop enmeshed in the daily work of the conference, lurching from one crisis to the next, micromanaging, has no time for strategic thinking.

At the end of a long day of administration, when I descended to my study to translate a sermon by Barth or read Wesley, it was a renewing vacation from the rigors of management. In advocating "self-differentiation" Friedman surprisingly cited "empathy" as an enemy of transformative systems leadership. Friedman charges that "the introduction of . . . 'empathy' into family, institutional, and community meetings" is "an effort to induce a failure of nerve among its leadership."[22]

In the church, "compassion" is used to defeat nerve. My first autumn as a bishop, a wise old pastor told me, "I think you are a gift to us. But I worry that you will grow to like us, to befriend us, and, as you do, you will become less effective in helping us. Be careful! We Alabamians will charm you into complete ineffectiveness."

The most important task for a district superintendent is to overcome the clerical propensity toward empathy. Thus, in interviewing candidates for DS, I asked, "Were any of your teenagers rebellious, immature, manipulative, dependent, or otherwise irresponsible?"

If the prospective DS said, "No. I have two wonderful kids who never ran afoul of the law," my countenance would fall and I would say, "I was hoping you had more experience in tough parenting; that would be helpful in your supervision of some of our passive-aggressive, immature clergy."

I spent much of my first two years asking my Cabinet questions like, "Why do you do it this way? Have you gotten the results you wanted? Would you like to think about a way to get different results?"

The longer I was bishop, the fewer questions I asked, which led to a concomitant diminishment of my effectiveness. I had gone native, betraying Jesus' warning to be in but not of the world (Rom. 12:2). Empathy had rendered me part of the problem, a producer and, therefore, a defender of the status quo.

Empathy causes clergy to go limp. One of the most debilitating aspects of COB meetings is our recent practice of devoting a vast amount of time cloistered in small "covenant groups." These support groups have no connection to any "covenant" to which I have assented. Their purpose is to provide an opportunity for bishops to compare notes on surgeries and health crises, become closer friends, and bellyache.[23]

In our therapeutic culture, when friendship and personal support are exercised without any theological control, the group becomes coercive. Being an affectionate, empathetic, and caring member of the group becomes more important than truth or results. Too often an appeal to "relationship" is code for: (1) the purpose of your ministry is to maintain harmony with me, (2) harmony with me is a higher purpose than the mission of Jesus, (3) do not violate the niceness boundary and threaten my comfort.

On three occasions, when I have decided to take some action contrary to the ethos of the COB, such as declining to go to an expensive meeting in Mozambique, I was warned, "This will damage your relationship with your fellow bishops," as if intragroup relationship is the purpose of the episcopacy. I've watched too many congregations wither because they have limited their ministry to the care, feeding, and concord of members.[24] The best part about the COB is being forced to convoke with the Africans. I arrive at the COB, lamenting that *episcope* actually requires work, lusting for a week of self-care (i.e., leisure) but after a conversation with bishops Joaquina Nhanala, Eben Nhiwatiwa, or David Yemba, hearing what they're up against, I say, "I don't have any problems."

Empathy is too low a goal for ministry of Word and sacrament. We therefore need to spend less time asking, "How are we feeling?" and more time asking, "Why are we here?" I terminated my Cabinet's practice of beginning our meetings with a hospital list—reporting on the health problems of our clergy and their families. Not that such problems are unimportant, it is rather that in the church such concerns tend to become preoccupations that allow empathy to trump every other concern—such as commitment to the mission of Jesus Christ and fruitfulness of ministry. When Jesus miraculously healed people, he often charged them not to make it a big deal—Jesus is about a greater mission even than health.

My twenty-eight-year-old assistant kidded me, saying, "You never receive any messages from the COB office except those that deal with the surgery, accidents, and health needs of aging bishops." It was true. Most communication from the COB is related to the physical deterioration of bishops. Is it news that older adults like me have health problems? Genesis squelched our lust for immortality at the first. I long for the day when we will receive an e-mail from the secretary of the council saying, "Pray for Bishop Willimon. He has just finished another meeting where he was unprepared and fell flat on his face. Pray that he will stay depressed about his performance long enough either to change or to resign."

Bishops are "overseers." We over-see. If we are too mired in the muck in the trenches, we do a poor job directing the course of the battle. While bishops serve within the bounds of an annual conference, it's a gift that we are sent there from beyond the conference. We are officers of the general church, we serve on General Conference boards and agencies, and we are paid (to put it crudely) by the General Conference, not by an annual conference. It is empowering that all UMC clergy, including bishops, while we must have ways of acquiring deep knowledge of our assigned location, also come from elsewhere and eventually depart. While there's much to be said for longer pastorates, bishops demonstrate the value of short, focused pastorates in which we lead God's work and then hightail it out of town. The desire for permanence, enduring legacy, longevity, and eternality are aspirations unworthy of those who work with a living, peripatetic, itinerate, chorietic Trinity.

Early in my episcopacy I made a decision to limit my work within the GC. I was offered membership on COSROW, but having just read a copy of their newsletter, I said that such service could make me suicidal. There was so much that needed doing in my assigned annual conference; I heard from so many that "you bishops need to stay home," that I focused most of my first quadrennial energies in the annual conference.

Now, I'm not so sure. There is much to be said for staying at home; there may be even more to be said for being away from home enough to foster critical perspective on home. What needs to happen in the General Conference happens first in each annual conference. I'm pleased that the Call to Action urges the COB to hold us accountable for fruitfulness in leading our conferences.

In order better to focus on that which is most essential, the COB must discipline itself not to issue public pronouncements and not to create programs and emphases as if the annual conferences are incapable of being faithful to Christ's ministry without prodding from the COB. Top-down pronouncements and programs are only relatively important and distract us from the absolutely essential—making more disciples. It is demeaning to conceive of the annual conference, in the benighted hinterland, awaiting the GC to think up areas of ministry for us.

Still, as bishop I'm an officer of the church at large. While I tend to be overwhelmed by all that needs doing in the General Conference (that is, all that needs *un*doing), the good news is that most of what needs doing also needs doing in the annual conference. My little nonsystemic, parochial brain can't figure out how to make the acronymic and archaic COSROW, GBCS, GCORR, or GBHM effective. While I commend the CTA's scathing criticism of our boards and agencies and support radical reductions, I leave such work to better, more doggedly persistent organizational minds than mine.[25] Fortunately, the activation of our boards and agencies is unnecessary to our future as a faithful church.

Knowing the date of my retirement lends urgency to my leadership. I began my episcopacy saying, "Studies show that our pastors need to stay in place longer. A pastor's most effective year is the sixth year." I now say not that we need longer pastorates but that we need pastorates to be more effective. For some that means digging in, expending a significant segment of life in service to a church; for others it means a short pastorate where a pastor blows in, tells truth, leads the congregation in difficult work that it has been avoiding for years, and then itinerates somewhere else.

My greatest appointive mistakes were not those pastors I recklessly moved but those pastors embedded in a congregational culture, so unused to itinerancy, which I cowardly failed to move. I urged our Cabinet to get better at diagnosing when a pastor and congregation have reached a plateau and when both pastor and congregation could benefit from the disruption and discombobulation of a move. For this sort of assessment, the Dashboard is invaluable. The Holy Spirit loves not only to induce dislocation but also to take advantage of the fresh starts and needed endings that the UM itinerancy provides.[26]

I lamented to a DS that the episcopacy committee seemed so willing for me to retire. He consoled me with, "Look. Eight years is all we can take. Be here just long enough to push us forward but not long enough to take responsibility from us. This is our work and we've got to own it if it is to be sustained. Have a nice retirement."

I would quibble with Rabbi Friedman's "self-differentiated" leader image in this one way—bishops, like all UM clergy, are "*God*-differentiated." We must be detached enough from the church to be heavily invested in the church *in Jesus' name*. All of us, wherever we serve, are just passing through, held accountable to a boss who is greater than the fickle, totalitarian praise or blame of the congregation.

My preparation for being an appropriately God-differentiated bishop was four decades as a preacher of the Word. Preachers are called to tell the truth, the truth which is Jesus Christ. Opposition, resistance, and negative response come with the job. Bishop Schnase advised episcopal aspirants, "You better have a high threshold of pain, because those who resist your efforts have multiple ways of discomforting you." Thus I told my superintendents on our first retreat, "You must never lie, not only because lying is wrong, but because we are preachers and lying is the death of gospel preaching." And in the church, lies are always told for the most noble of empathetic, caring reasons.

My conference has benefited from the tools of natural church development, specifically the NCD inventory that enables a congregation to see their "minimum" and their "maximum" factors. Through the NCD inventory, for the first time many of these congregations are facing the truth.

Ronald Heifetz said, "When an organization calls you a 'leader,' those in authority reward you for doing what they want you to do and punish you for changing things in ways that require them to work differently or that threaten their world view."[27]

In the early days of my episcopacy, when a retired pastor spent an hour of lambasting me for "ruining our conference," and other grievances, I responded, "I doubted I was accomplishing anything. Your anger certifies that I'm actually having an impact, changing more than I thought. Why else would you be so threatened? Thanks for confirming my effectiveness."

As a preacher, I'm accustomed to having to speak unpleasant truth from the pulpit in the name of Jesus. There's no way for truth to be bad because (1) God intends for us to know the truth about God and ourselves, and (2) God has given us what we need to be transformed, to grow, to move more dynamically into the future—if we will avail ourselves of God-given opportunities for transformation.

I began this chapter by admitting that sometimes the church and its bishops function as a perverse defense against the disruptive intrusions of the Holy Spirit. I end by asserting that the sovereign Holy Spirit can work anywhere it pleases, including through bishops and *The Book of Discipline*. The Heaths say that leading change requires "open minds, creativity, and hope,"[28] in short, just the sort of virtues instilled in us through encounters with the living Christ. Christians are forced into change, conversion, and transformation, not because the poor old church is stuck, but because we are stuck with Jesus. Flaccid liberal Christianity, the predominant theological mode of The UMC, jettisoned the eschatological dimensions of the gospel. We are now paying dearly as a church for our theological mistake, so content are we with the present, fearful to venture because we have lost the eschatological perspective that is the wellspring of Christian hope. Christ is eschatological, dismantling the present, never content, projecting us beyond the merely now into God's promised future, a future in which God, while not dependent on us, graciously enlists us, telling us the secret about where we're all headed once God finally gets what God wants. Therefore, we do not lose hope.

At lunch after service in a small, rural congregation, a couple of retired schoolteachers offhandedly told me about their after-school program for latchkey kids. "Turned out that most of 'em spoke Spanish. Had to get Lillian here" (she said, pointing to an older woman at the next table) "to teach us Spanish. Baptized two." There, in that church hall, over fried chicken, I saw a new heaven and a new earth.

CHAPTER SIX

BISHOPS BODY BUILDING

Young Francis of Assisi wandered into the abandoned chapel of San Damiano in his hometown one afternoon to speak with God. To his surprise God talked to him through a crucifix: "Francis, rebuild my church that you see is falling down." Impulsive Francis began repairs on a dilapidated, unused chapel.

I visited San Damiano as a college student on a cold January day and got a reproduction of the talking crucifix that has hung on the wall of my study ever since, now next to my picture, from the *Arminian Magazine*, of John Wesley. Of course, I'm neither Francis nor Father John, but they are reminders to me that if you're not into rebuilding, reconstruction, and renovation, never accept leadership in the Body of Christ. Church is a mess—and always has been. Thus the Lord graciously leaves something for us to do, enlisting us to rebuild the church.

My first month in Birmingham, a layperson led me on a tour of McCoy UMC, just across from my office on the Birmingham-Southern campus. McCoy's large, Methodist neo-Gothic building is now empty except for our small senior care ministry. We walked through abandoned Sunday school rooms, watched pigeons fluttering in the rafters of the littered sanctuary.

Eleven months later I marched the annual conference from the auditorium at Birmingham-Southern in a procession out the campus gate, across the street to McCoy. There I led the conference in prayers of repentance and commitment, repenting of the racism and insularity that led to the closing of this inner-city church, and committed to get back in contact with the community we had abandoned.[1]

After surveying two hundred years of American Methodist bishops, Russ Richey said that we bishops have personified three necessary functions for our church: *teacher, exemplar,* and *architect.*[2] Teacher, exemplar, yes, these are historic functions of the *episcope.* But architect?

United Methodism is in great part the construction of bishops. Just as Coke and Asbury had to devise the ecclesial structures required to enact the Wesleyan vision in North America, so bishops now must lead in the evaluation, critique, and creation of the architecture of our church.[3] In the present age it is insufficient for bishops to efficiently care for the church; we must rebuild the church that is forever reformed and reforming, working from Christ's mandate to the church toward a rigorous refurbishment of the church so that we might, in our time and place, more faithfully work with Christ.

I give thanks that I got to be a bishop at a time when our church is undergoing some life-giving, gospel-induced reconstruction that required me to be an architect, or at least a renovator. Interior decoration or minor repairs are no longer enough. Any new vision must but build upon the foundation established.[4] Leaders of sustainable change are retrofitters rather than bulldozers, recovering an identity that is peculiarly, indicatively Wesleyan.[5]

TRUTH NOW

I thought that every Methodist church would beat on my door, pleading, "Help! We're failing and you have got to send us the pastors we need to be more faithful!"

To my chagrin, the culture of contentment, more honestly, a culture of denial and avoidance, was my greater challenge.

To be fair, we have spent decades teaching congregations that the pastoral leadership we send them is the best they should unquestioningly expect, decline is their unavoidable fate, and the church they have is the best God can do.

Some management consultants say that leaders must never cry "Crisis!" and that there is value in a leader's "nonanxious presence." Here I want to say a word for anxiety. In the three decades in which we lost 20 percent of our strength, we made not one major change in the way our church functions. My conference discussed downsizing the number of our districts for *forty years.* Finally, when the annual conference acknowledged that we had the same number of district superintendents serving forty thousand fewer Methodists, in six months we went from twelve to eight. (Two years later, during a severe financial crisis, I had one DS serve two urban districts at great savings without diminution of mission.)

Praise God the jurisdictional episcopacy committee sent me to North Alabama where I was greeted by enough people who said, "We are unhappy with our current results and think that God has sent you to enable us to do better." My predecessor, Bob Fannin, in stressing evangelism, gave me a great gift by having created a culture of discontent. All I did was to find a way to measure our evangelistic efforts and to note those pastors who had demonstrated gifts for leading evangelization.

True, we had naysayers. A group of retired clergy agitated for my removal after my first quadrennium. Removal would have been a difficult task to accomplish even for the most dedicated of my detractors because of the system's safeguards for bishops and the lethargy of the jurisdictional episcopacy committee. Any Methodist preacher attempting to be bishop must quickly be cured of a desire to please. If the architectural work that needs doing in our church were easy, it would have been done six bishops ago. During my first year alone I received communications saying that I was "destroying the church I love." One letter compared me to both King George and Hitler. And those were critics who were courageous enough to tell me what they thought, unlike the cowards at the Monday morning preacher's coffee hour sob session.

People fear change because they fear loss. When Patsy and I returned to the episcopal residence one afternoon to find our home trashed and everything of value ripped off, including the collection of coins I inherited from my grandfather for whom I was named, I was in grief. That evening it dawned on me why I was receiving angry pushback from some of my pastors: I was a thief, robbing them of the church that once comforted and protected them, ripping off their treasured inheritance.

Nearly all transformative leadership books give advice on how to handle resistance and criticism, but none speak about the peculiar Christian command to love the enemy. "You have heard that it was said, 'You shall love your neighbor and hate your enemy.' But I say to you, Love your enemies and pray for those who persecute you" (Matt. 5:43-48). A bishop without enemies must not be showing up at the office. Church is a grand arena to attempt enemy love. I'd rather love Iranian Shiites any day; I don't have to try to be the Body of Christ with them. The struggle to love your opponents as Jesus loves, to resist the temptation to bear false witness against them, to believe that they love the church as much as I, even if differently, are among the challenges of loving UM enemies.

Enemy love may be particularly difficult in a United Methodist Church that assumes that we have concocted a form of flaccid and inoffensive Christianity that nobody—except for wicked, deeply evil people—could hate us. No, wherever Jesus is busy, his work brings enemies out of the woodwork, some of whom are more adept practitioners of the gospel than I. None of the baptized is excused from his command to love our enemies, least of all the ones who are commissioned to be "examples to the flock."

Retired DSs, other bishops confirm, tend to be a bishop's most severe critics—those who have given much to work an unworkable system do not applaud those who dismantle that system. To our few embittered retired clergy I simply pled, "While I can understand how what we are attempting is a threat to the world that you defended, please believe that we are sincerely attempting to be faithful to Christ in our time and place. Pray that it will bear fruit for the future."[6]

I also found it helpful (after a particularly spiteful meeting in which half a dozen retired clergy took turns criticizing me and Patsy) to spend the next week praying for each critic by name.

Retired clergy who are old enough to remember when our church actually grew were some of our most encouraging supporters. Clergy and lay leaders who have served our church from 1969 (the night I was ordained) until 2011 (the eve of my retirement) have experienced nothing but decline, the only decline in our more than two centuries as a church, and find it difficult to imagine church on the move.

I lament the precipitous rise in the average age of our clergy because I believe that younger clergy have the least patience with our dysfunctional systems and are the most likely to have skills to reach a new generation. Impatience and impetuousness, both youthful virtues, are gifts The UMC now desperately needs. I don't recall anybody accusing Father John of being cautious and circumspect before attempting innovation. He couldn't have learned incaution at Oxford; it must have been a fruit of the Holy Spirit.

Ken Blanchard said that in order to foster a sense of urgency a leader must bring people face-to-face with the truth of their situation.[7] Fortunately for The UMC, we have got the numbers. Unfortunately, we have too many people who seem to think that their job is to obfuscate the numbers. Fortunately, I not only have the truth-telling function of the North Alabama Conference Dashboard, but I'm also a preacher; I'm ordained to tell the truth on a weekly basis. When Paul calls the church "the body of Christ" (1 Cor. 12:12-31), it means that it is not the church that tells Christians who Jesus is; Jesus' words and deeds tell us what the church is. We don't know the truth of our situation until we hear it from Jesus, who is the way, the life, and the truth.

Generally speaking, the conference leaders whom a bishop inherits will not be the leaders a bishop needs. God has given us everyone we need in order to go forward, though a mediocre, moribund administration of an otherwise noble ecclesiastical system has pushed many of them to the margins. A bishop therefore must pray for the grace to see the human resources that God has given and invite and empower them to lead. A good place to look for innovative clergy leaders is among the ranks of our clergy-women and our younger pastors, who may have been passed over by a system that privileges seniority, years of service, gender, stability, or other non-gospel concerns over the mission of the church.

Leaders foster change by asking, "Why do you do it this way?" and "Are you getting the results you want?" and "Would you like to think together on another way of doing this?" As a new bishop, devoid of experience, wisdom, and skills to do the work, unsure of what the work was, I was forced to ask for help at each turn in the road. A couple of years into the job, I began to think I actually knew something. I asked fewer questions. I was beginning to regard the status quo as normal; I was part of the problem. So I intentionally conducted discussions with groups of lay leaders, effective church staffs, and young adults in our younger congregations. I got a fresh appreciation for the additional work that we needed to do.

One reason I answered all correspondence, even the most critical (including the avalanche of letters dumped on me when I sued our legislature over the immigration bill), is that some of the critical letters were also truthful. One young adult told me of visiting four congregations before she received a personal response from anyone. Her letter gave me my assignment for the week.

Historian Gary Wills said that if you are a white, male Southerner over fifty (and I am), there is no way to convince you that people cannot change. Having experienced radical transformation of heart and mind within your own family, deep within your own soul, you have an unshakable belief in the possibility of human alteration. I kept telling the Methodists of Alabama that our not-too-distant past was a great impetus for change in the present. Every year I made pilgrimage to the Civil Rights Institute in Birmingham, walked past the displays of our recent, violent past, and was emboldened to believe afresh that God can take our evil and make it God's good. Of course, it's also edifying for a leader to be reminded of all the people who did not change but sat on the sidelines, attempting to preserve the old world rather than enjoy one of the Holy Spirit's great interventions in history.

Constantly inviting new people to the Cabinet, always asking for help and being surprised by whom God sends, disciplining oneself to ask questions before offering answers, readily admitting failure, spending most time with the church's most productive people, refusing to be held captive by failure, helps a bishop preserve amateur status before the eyes of God.

CHURCH IN MOTION

Because the church is Christ's Body, the church is not incidental or inconsequential to our salvation. If we are going to be saved by God in Jesus Christ, we must avail ourselves of the God-ordained means of salvation—the poor old, compromised tart whom Jesus believes to be his beloved bride. Our soteriology (doctrine of salvation) is therefore tethered to our ecclesiology (doctrine of the church). To those who say we lack a full-orbed ecclesiology, we Wesleyans—a movement before we were a church—say that our critics' ecclesiologies may be too static; Methodism is church in motion. The Body of Christ atrophies when it is a parochial, static body in residence, preoccupied with self-care. Resisting the ever-present clerical temptation to be care-givers and managers of an institution, we are "mission movers."[8] We no longer go out to do mission work elsewhere in a pleasantly Christian America; we call and equip people to be missionaries in an essentially pagan North American mission field. Laity are called, not to keep up the church, but to be part of the mission of

Jesus Christ in the world. The shift from an America of Constantinian Christendom has been under way at least since Stanley Hauerwas and I named it in *Resident Aliens*[9]; the future for the church is in recovering its core—a countercultural, communal movement empowered by the Holy Spirit that enables people, in service to Jesus Christ, to resist the wiles of the world.

Our great task is not to stabilize, standardize, or harmonize the People of God but rather to be the church in motion.[10] Jesus Christ is God on the move and the structures of Methodism should be the bare organizational essentials that are required to keep disciples moving. Bishop Asbury would want me to say that sending people out as missionaries precedes bringing people in as members. Social justice and evangelism are the same movement: Jesus' "come unto me" linked to Jesus' "go into all the world." Today it is more important to experience agitation by the wild, untamed, uncontained power of the Holy Spirit than it is to control by denominational rules and structures. An experience of the liveliness of the risen Christ is more important than a set of uniformly enforced ways of being the church. God give us more bishops whose idea of a good time is to be on the back of a motorcycle at ninety miles an hour.

In order to be a church on the move we are shifting our middle judicatory responsibility (the work of DSs) away from conflict resolution to intervention and coaching. It is more important for a pastor to prod and empower than to pacify. *Conflict* (from the Latin, *confligere*, "to start a fire") is an expected, necessary by-product of transformative leadership in the name of Jesus. The church begins (Acts 2) in fire and earth trembling; the church dies by rules and regulations. As a connectional church, those of us in the ministry of oversight must do more proactive intervention (troublemaking) in which we tell the truth to a congregation about its present dilemma, show them what they must do to have a vital future, obtain the pastoral leadership to lead these strategies, and then monitor them and hold them accountable to respond to Christ-induced agitation.[11] Our pastors must be trained and held accountable as mission leaders rather than as caregivers. Our laity must be transformed from being enablers of the narcissistic, immature behavior of passive receivers of ministry into apostles where each person, in baptism, is sent as minister.

Bishops need not concern ourselves with boringly institutional concerns like seniority, stability, continuity, order, process, uniformity, and consensus; it's time to worry about what the Trinity thinks about our church. Those of us at the top of the hierarchy must relinquish need for control and bless a certain amount of holy chaos and apostolic risk-taking by the faithful as they experiment with new forms of mission to learn again the delight of working with a resurrected Savior and a pushy Holy Spirit who love to revolutionize through the meek and lowly.

One of the great blessings of being a bishop today is that we have more reliable, tested help for church revitalization than we have had in a century—NCD, fruitful practices, a host of proven consultants, and a new generation of pastors, bishops, and DSs who see themselves as leaders of growth rather than managers of decline. A bishop must not only reach out for and coordinate help but also note well those clergy and churches who are unable or unwilling to receive help. Every church that fully participated in our NCD program grew; every one of our churches in decline was served by pastors who lack the skill to utilize NCD. Invariably, if a church finds it impossible to send a meager 10 percent of its income to connectional giving (apportionments), that church is being underserved by a pastor who has refused to take advantage of our training in stewardship leadership.

No bishop is required to compensate for mediocrity in our churches and clergy. Early Methodist circuit riders were the elite, Jesuits of Protestant Christianity. It's sad when our contemporary church fails to call its best talent into service to and leadership of the church or thinks so little of its mission that it fails to remove the inept and incompetent.

A DS bragged that he was spending a couple of hours a week meeting with one of his young clergy, trying to help her preaching. If someone has been to seminary for three years, taken two preaching courses from a professor of homiletics, and still is unable to achieve minimum levels of homiletic proficiency, doesn't this suggest that the DS's time would be better spent exiting this pastor? Excessive need for teaching and training are often indicators that those of us in oversight have appointed the wrong person. In Jim Collins's words, we put the wrong person on the bus. Our empathy for misplaced, untalented pastors must be trumped by our empathy for poorly led, underserved congregations.

Years ago Lyle Schaller told us that United Methodism had found a perverse way to reward our failures and to punish our successes, entrenching mediocrity and ignoring excellence. We must honor success in missional leadership rather than reward loyalty to the system. Again, the seniority system is nowhere encouraged by our *Discipline* but is everywhere strangling us. Wesley made the scandalous move to utilize lay preachers because of (1) his single-minded, practical commitment to the mission of Jesus Christ, and (2) his high doctrine of the Holy Spirit. Contemporary "traveling preachers" need less job security and more reassurance that if a pastor is effective and productive, we will fully utilize that pastor's God-given ability without regard to worldly labels of race, gender, or age.

We expend missional resources to subsidize decline and death. Equitable compensation and other subsidies ought to be abandoned in favor of offering short-term, accountable seed money to those churches that are clearly on our vanguard of missional change. Subsidies debilitate a church and protect bishops from having to make painful decisions. We have some annual conferences that waste nearly a million dollars every year for EC. These funds are not being used for the short-term, missional purpose that is directed by the *Discipline* (¶¶624-25) but rather to prop up the salaries of ineffective elders who are unable to grow a congregation. In other words, EC is being abused to protect bishops and cabinets from having to make tough decisions about ineffective pastors.

To the collective shame of all of us in oversight in our conference, when we finally exited two of our ineffective pastors, just before their retirement, the two of them walked away with a million dollars of EC funds. I should have been fired for taking six years to accomplish the exit of such dramatically incompetent elders. My Cabinet courageously decided to go "cold turkey" on EC and to solve problems with unproductive clergy and shrinking congregations by other means. That one decision forced us to work more faithfully.

A seminal insight of Lyle Schaller is that our church subsidizes and produces small, unproductive, static congregations and punishes growing, large congregations.[12] Schaller reported "an increase in the number reporting an average attendance of 19 or fewer from 3,839 in 1972 to 4,688 at the end of 2001, and a decrease in the number averaging 100 or more at worship from 11,689 in 1972 to 9,925 at the end of 2001."[13]

One of Bishop Hunt's six keys to insuring a future for The UMC was "We must assure the survival of the small membership church."[14] If he were still with us, I would reassure Bishop Hunt that he need not have worried about the small membership UMC. We have more small membership churches than any other denomination in Christendom for one reason—bishops. By privileging these churches, we mask the truth that most of them are in decline for two reasons: (1) For the past sixty years Americans have not been attracted to small congregations;[15] (2) churches decline when they withdraw from obedience to Jesus as seen in Matthew 28.

I could not understand the anger and hurt that was directed at me by members of some of these congregations: "The conference is killing our small churches with the burden of apportionments." In truth the bishop and the Cabinet are the sole reason for so many small churches in the UMC—we send trained, dedicated pastors to churches who, were they part of any other denomination, would be unable to attract this level of leadership and would have closed long ago.

We have allowed small, declining, insular congregations to dominate our denomination. Our 25 largest churches have over 83,000 people in weekly worship, with an average of 3,346 people in each congregation (these 25 churches welcome more Methodists in worship each week than the total worship attendance of 54 out of 62 annual conferences!).[16]

Fortunately, we Wesleyans are heirs of a tradition that contains within it the memory of a stuffy little Oxford don who was transformed by the in-breaking grace of God and thereby ignited a spiritual awakening that transformed a moribund church. Remembrance that we've done it before can be a catalyst to doing it again.

LOVING THE BODY

In April of 1931, Dietrich Bonhoeffer traveled through Alabama on old Highway 11 with fellow seminarian Frank Fisher (son of C. L. Fisher, pastor of Birmingham's famous 16th Street Baptist Church).[17] Bonhoeffer, a twenty-four-year-old theological prodigy (whose work Karl Barth called "miraculous") had never met a person of African descent. Traveling with Fisher exposed this brilliant German to American racism. They sailed down segregated Highway 11 the same month the Scottsboro Boys were taken off a train and arrested.

When he was my guest at Duke Chapel, Bonhoeffer biographer Eberhard Bethge told me, "America changed Bonhoeffer." Returning to Berlin in the fall of 1931, Bonhoeffer said that his American sojourn "grounded his theology in reality." His theology took on new urgency in its attention to the outcast and reviled. He engaged in a fresh reading of the Sermon on the Mount, interpreting it in an almost Wesleyan way. No longer did this Lutheran speak of grace as a one-sided, heaven-sent act from God, but as a divine partnership with humanity.

I like to believe that Bonhoeffer's time in Alabama was a key to his theological move. While I'm no Bonhoeffer, I confess that before being bishop in Alabama, much of my theology lacked concreteness. My job in Alabama forced me to practice Wesleyan "practical divinity"—either to put my theory into action, or else to admit its stupidity. It is of primary importance to ask the theological "Why are we in ministry?" but it is of equal theological importance for us Wesleyans to ask, "*How* will we *do* ministry?"[18]

The practical, performed, corporate embodiment of the faith is the task that God has assigned Wesleyanism. Ken Carder and Laceye Warner said that our church needs "foundation repair," requiring "patience and perseverance and a willingness to get one's hands dirty and work without recognition and immediate visible results."[19] Those who dismiss concerns over the fruitfulness of our UMC systems as mere "tinkering with structure" haven't read our history. From our first days as a church, the Methodist movement was conservative in replicating orthodox Anglican doctrine and radically innovative in creating new structure.

Docetism is an ever-present temptation, the notion that Christ only appeared to be human. Chalcedonian faith means that God comes to us as Christ, bone of our bone, flesh of our flesh, God too close for comfort. In the Incarnation, God refused to stop short of our humanity. God's truth became actual in our space and time, the eternal Word became creature. Church is the scandalously human, too-specific-for-evasion way that Christ continues to incarnate.

In the 1970s, we United Methodists organized ourselves on the (already outdated) model of corporate America.[20] Our rule-driven, legislatively dominated common life as a denomination make references to The UMC as "family" sound hollow. In too many ways we are The UMC, Inc., with our stress upon regulation, legislation, governance by committee, and our voluminous (required but unread) reports and enforced uniform compliance throughout all segments of the corporation—I mean, *connection*.

In this book, I have drawn upon the insights of systems analysis and organizational theory from business. Am I exchanging one

101

form of godless commercial organization for another? Church history shows that sometimes, in baptizing secular practices, the world subverts us and we betray gospel foolishness for merely worldly wisdom.

I defend my interest in the work of people like Heifetz and Rendle by saying that our UMC problem, in our present structures, is that we are organized for purposes (death, caregiving, maintenance, self-protection) that are not only inappropriate for the church's mission at our time and place but also incongruent with the primary mission of the church (growth, risk, service, outreach, transformation).

Dean Greg Jones of Duke noted that our great need is not for more good ideas for our church but rather "execution with urgency." He said that "because we think the ideas matter so much . . . we pay comparatively little attention to how we implement those ideas, and whether the organizations we create to embody our ideas will themselves be generative."[21] I agree.

Our church behaves as if the greatest challenge is top-down control and far-flung representation—the maximum number of diverse groups represented, giving maximum input in every decision.[22] Groups jockey for recognition in the *Discipline*, boards and agencies spend more energy designating who will be at the discussion than the mission to which the discussions should contribute. Even as I write this, our boards and agencies are engaged in their quadrennial exercise of maneuvering in a shrinking general church budget instead of asking, "Why are we here and what ought to be expected of us?"

The Call to Action seems to agree with Lyle Schaller that two of the biggest shortcomings in our denomination are "the absence of an executive office or branch in both the annual conferences and the national structure, and the absence of a publically reported annual performance audit."[23] We are on the way, if we are faithful to the CTA, to a restoration both of an active executive office and publically reported performance. These mundane systemic changes will produce spiritual fruit.

Wesley worried about the lapse of Methodism in which we retained the *"form"* of the faith without the *"power."* Wesleyan power was not our power to build a thriving organization or even to do good things for the suffering world. It was the power of God at work in the world in raising up the People Called Methodists. If this book is a mere meditation on form, as important as form is in an incarnational faith, without sufficient attention to the divinely given empowerment that enlivens and gives birth to form, we validate Wesley's worries. The way to have deep experiences of the Holy Spirit is not to ignore form but to come up with those forms that are uniquely suited to people of the Spirit.

James Dittes, my teacher of pastoral care, long ago called administration the great pastoral scapegoat, that which we pastors do in order to keep from doing the more threatening tasks of ministry like preaching and enacting the gospel of Jesus Christ.[24] Bishops are not immune from the temptation to make ministry easier than Jesus means ministry to be by focusing on the mechanics rather than the mission. It is safer to keep the machinery oiled than to obey the explosive promptings of the Holy Spirit.

Still, one of the great intellectual, theological challenges was to be a bishop who not only loved the Body of Christ but also was called to the service of edifying the Body of Christ. For all of Saint Paul's high-flown theology, his main concern, his main test of all spiritual gifts, was edification of the Body. That's the supreme test for the work of a bishop too.

LOVING INSTITUTIONS

A major way that a bishop cares for the church is by caring for the church's far-flung institutions. I was plopped on *twelve* boards of trust—three colleges, a complex of children's homes, a network of homes for the elderly, a clergy continuing education foundation, superannuate homes for retired pastors, the Methodist Foundation, a camp/retreat center, a statewide interfaith coalition, and the United Methodist Women, not counting the boards and agencies in which I participated for the general church (in my case chairing the Study on Ministry, presiding over the Theological Education Commission of the University Senate, and being a member of the Committee on Faith and Order). Only the president of Emory, Jim Wagner, came to me with a good argument for why I should be on his board (we need someone who has spent his life in Christian higher education). All the rest urged me to be on the board because the bishop before me was on the board. I even chaired a bankrupt hospital (any hospital that makes a bishop chair of the board will be bankrupt sooner or later). They closed in six months.

Some of these boards (the United Methodist Women, for instance) have a bishop on board as a quaint relic from the past to give them the illusion that they are actually functioning in the present—we must be doing something right; see the bishop there, dozing quietly at our meeting. My attempts to challenge the UMW to reach out to a new generation of United Methodist women were shunned. Any institution that puts a bishop on their board is probably continuing a practice that harkens back to the days when the church was a major supporter of these institutions and bishops had the luxury of sitting through hours of meetings and, save for the opening prayer, contributed little.

Most of my board activity related to the three educational institutions under my purview—Emory University (exceedingly well-managed, financially solvent), Huntingdon College (where I learned from visionary Pastor-President Cam West, who worked a dramatic turnaround), and Birmingham-Southern College (which I bewilderingly watched atrophy before my eyes). My service to these educational institutions was aligned with my previous experience. (I'm the only bishop anyone remembers who was summoned from campus ministry to the episcopacy.) Patsy and I funded endowed lectureships or scholarships at all three colleges in a small attempt better to link the church to higher education.

Bishop Hope Morgan Ward put our challenge well when she said, "We bishops have complete responsibility and virtually no authority in matters of oversight of our church's institutions." Birmingham-Southern's troubles will long be lamented in the annals of higher education as a tragic instance of a good college brought to the brink by bad governance. Birmingham-Southern enjoyed the most deeply affectionate church-college relationship of any college in the connection. I inherited a four-and-a-half-million-dollar Methodist Center that is in the middle of the beautiful BSC campus, the finest office for a bishop and conference anywhere in The UMC. BSC is our conference's largest in-state recipient of funds, all of which go to scholarships for Methodist students. Because one of our conference priorities was reaching a new generation of UM Christians, I taught once a year at BSC, a course in contemporary theology (from which I gleaned four of our best young pastors) as well as a yearly course, Jesus through the Centuries (out of which I wrote a book on Jesus, dedicated to students at BSC).

BSC's hotshot new president arrived in town the same week as I. He said at an early public meeting, "I was so glad to see that Will Willimon was coming here as bishop because now I've got someone else to be the lightning rod and catch the heat." He meant that as a compliment. When two BSC students burned nine rural churches to the ground in my second year as bishop, our president led magnificently, church and college working together to rebuild the churches.

Unfortunately, the president's financial leadership was not as adept. At our board meeting in May of 2010 the president again reassured us that all was well at BSC and that we were, despite the country's worst recession, moving ahead with new dorms, faculty raises, a football stadium, and a classy lake behind the Methodist Center. Two weeks later it was announced that we had financial irregularities. The executive committee of the board began to meet behind closed doors. In July the college announced the termination of more than fifty employees, including twenty faculty, the termination of four majors, and other drastic cuts—without board consultation.

In August I wrote an open letter to the board demanding a thorough airing of our true situation. We had our board meeting in which it was disclosed that the crisis was much, much deeper than we had been told, not a couple of million but many millions in shortfall this year alone, that we had spent down the college's endowment by over half (the lectureship that Patsy and I had given was gone), and we were in a life-and-death fight for the survival of our college.

A group of faculty urged me to step up, "save the college," (some of the same faculty who had spent their lives attempting to distance themselves from the church!) and help exit the president (when the panicked faculty couldn't come up with a vote of no confidence). That week my assistant was told that my services would no longer be needed for teaching a class because of the financial cuts. I had been teaching the course gratis, giving back the paltry stipend to help fund our lectureship. BSC's culture of administrative concealment became more understandable—the managerial ineptitude was breathtaking.

I moved our conference in high gear to help the college. Our church prepaid (nearly two hundred thousand) our yearly apportionment to the college for scholarships, received a special offering, appealed to our one-hundred clergy alumni for help, offered one of our best young pastors to be chaplain, and after urging the president to leave, I served on the search committee to select a new president for BSC. No United Methodist could be found whom the faculty would accept as president. In a review in spring of 2011, our UM University Senate gave BSC a stinging public warning charging poor oversight by the board, bad decisions by the faculty, terrible internal management, a squandering of our inheritance, and betrayal of the church's trust.

Birmingham-Southern will be digging out for decades. The church is the best friend that the little college has, though I fear that the college abused its relationship to the church. BSC may join the ranks of all the United Methodist schools that once had a vital part in the mission of the church but now have lost connection to our mission. We closed four UM colleges while I was on our UM University Senate. The BSC episode proved to me the peculiar power of bishops and the necessity of active, close, careful oversight by a board for trust. My argument for bishops being discriminating about their board memberships is not that boards of trust are unimportant but that, in a declining, weakening system, boards of trust are too important to allow a seat on the board to be occupied by a half-hearted board member who probably has no expertise in financial and business management.

Generally speaking, few of our institutions need the help of a bishop—until they fall into desperate situations. Then suddenly a bishop is an important benefactor and is expected to step up and save the institution from its self-induced malaise. Methodism has built so many excellent institutions because our church has always exercised rather casual control over our hospitals, children's homes, schools, and colleges. Our nondominating relationship caused most of them to drift far from the church. And yet when their lives are threatened and they look for friends, they tend to fall into the arms of the church, even though they may have ceased being a vital part of the church's ministry.

The church must decide if these institutions are still part of our mission and if our shrinking resources should continue to be used in their behalf. About the only good news I could find in the situation of BSC was that the poor old church, for all our faults, is a so much better managed institution than our college that often felt itself superior to the church.

My first visit with the director and board of trustees of our beloved Camp Sumatanga filled me with fear; neither director nor board had a clue about how to help our camp survive. Attempting to reinvent themselves into a camp-retreat center, at a time when denominations were stuck with scores of bankrupt retreat centers, having amassed debt while neglecting needed capital improvements, both board and director seemed paralyzed. Their lack of comprehension of their current situation was confirmed by their expectation that somehow our shrinking conference could come up with the millions needed to bail them out.

I began a process of gently nudging the board, followed by attempts to shove and to kick the board. All that earned was the board's hurt and animosity. Suddenly the bishop was a bigger problem than the camp's aging sewer system.

In desperation I appointed a Bishop's Commission to Study Camp Sumatanga. Six businesspersons gave hours examining every aspect of the camp as a ministry that was also a business. They issued a report (that would have cost thousands if they had not been Methodists doing it gratis) that detailed what the camp needed to survive. I presented the report to the board. Two members of the board began crying, and one deeply offended board member charged me with a failure to love the camp as much as he loved the camp. The board refused to respond to the report.

Long story short, we were able to exit the director and gradually, all too gradually, to reconstitute the board. Enlisting the aid of retired Bishop Bob Morgan, we had a capital campaign—not much money raised; we have not had a successful capital campaign in our conference in decades, but we drew attention to the plight of the camp. I helped get a big grant from a foundation, the largest in the camp's history. We now have a top-notch UM businessperson (gratis) attempting to get this beloved but poorly managed facility back on its feet and positioned for future ministry.

One of the best things we bishops do is to call UM Christians to the ministry of oversight. One young man who spent hours working on the camp report thanked me for asking him to contribute so much unpaid expertise, telling me, "I'm an accountant, and this is the first time my church asked me to do anything which God gave me gifts to do."

When I hear fellow bishops brag about the hours they put in attempting to salvage a nursing home, our pension fund, or a college or camp from ruin, I think, "Is this simple arrogance—when hands were laid on my head, God made me an expert in all matters not only spiritual but also commercial and financial—or a tragic instance of a bishop robbing some fellow Christian of that person's baptismally bestowed ministry?"

Having received complaints about the management of our homes for the aging, I met with the board and attempted to get the homes to join the Methodist association that oversees and helps such facilities; the board told me that they were doing fine, thank you, and that I surely had more pressing matters with which to concern myself. I gave up.

Our church has a rapidly shrinking base. United Methodists of the past had a genius for organizing and building to beat the devil. That means that today's bishops spend much of their time administering yesterday's good ideas. We are stuck with hundreds of institutions, some of which are a tribute to the organizational genius of Wesleyan Christianity in America in the past, as well as others that suggest a bishop's inability to help the church face a painful truth, many of which won't make it another decade.

In my office I've got a wonderful picture of my dear mentor Kenneth Goodson. Ken led Alabama with distinction as bishop in the turbulent 1960s, coaxing the environs of "Bombingham" (as the civil rights movement dubbed my bishopric) into a more just society. When I enter my office to begin my daily work with bankrupt institutions dissolving before my eyes, I look at the picture and say, "Ken. You had it easier. All you had to contend with was bombs in your shrubbery and crosses being burned on your front yard."

Then Ken looks at me, in that contemptuous gaze that endeared him to so many and says, "My dear, young, dumb friend, closing and downsizing ministries that had invigorating purpose some time ago, realizing afresh that only God is eternal, helping ministries refocus, this also is service to a living Lord."

Martha Goodson gave me Ken's pulpit robe the day I was assigned to Alabama. I wear that mantle with reverence and delight throughout Alabama, playing Elisha to Ken's Elijah, a visible reminder of the grand, endless line of splendor that preceded me in this peculiar ministry. Bishops better than I preceded me, enduring hours sitting at tables in board meetings, attempting to love institutions, many of whom were unsure if they wanted to be loved by bishops.

By many people's estimate we have at least three seminaries that ought to be closed or merged. A 25-percent loss of membership calls for a concomitant downsizing of our administrative and support structures. Our seminaries are under stress simply because we have too many seminaries and too few quality faculty and students. The UMC has a rapidly shrinking need for seminary-trained elders—aggravated by the incapacity of our churches financially to support an elder's compensation and benefits. A major reason that my churches fail to pay their fair share of connectional giving is the increasing strain placed upon their dwindling budgets by the salaries of elders serving fewer Methodists.

Under my chairmanship the theological commission of the University Senate dramatically changed our formula for allocating ministerial education funds to the seminaries—aligning funding to the number of UM pastors the seminary actually educates. We also dropped some non-UM seminaries from our list of non-UMC seminaries approved to educate UM pastors.

Our remaining viable, well-functioning seminaries want to be held accountable for preparing the pastoral leaders that our church needs. Our seminaries are finally getting the point that we are a church in desperate need of a new breed of clerical leadership. Once again, bishops will be a key to better alignment of our resources. Rather than wait for more of our seminaries quietly to slip below the level of financial viability, or further to compromise their academic integrity by distributing our shrinking resources to too many institutions, the bishops must demand that our hard-won church financial resources are responsibly used.

The UMC is marvelously positioned—because of who we are and have been and where we are determined to go—to reach a new generation for Wesleyan Christianity. For instance, I admit to the doctrinal mushiness that sometimes infects us Methodists. And yet I realize that many young adults are suspicious of doctrinal dogmatism and rigidity. We've got a generation bored by and suspicious of institutions but a generation continuing to feel pursued by Jesus. Our heart-felt, open-handed, generous orthodoxy is just what they are dying for. For our determination to be the church for the sake of those outside the church, our practical determination to do what needs to be done to re-fit ourselves for ministry in a demanding time and place, it's a great time to be a UM Christian.

One unbearably hot Alabama-in-July day, I reluctantly made the drive out into the country to speak (reluctantly) to a mid-high camp gathering. The sweating, chigger-infested kids sat (reluctantly) before me. I gave them my thought for the week, looking at signs of camp decay all around me, thinking how peeved I was with the haphazard management by the camp board.

Afterward, on my way back down a rough, poorly lighted trail, a camper, whom I judged to be about eleven or so, hailed me in the darkness.

"Bishop, way to go. Liked your talk."

I thanked him and told him how I treasured a positive evaluation of my work by any adolescent.

"How has your week at camp been?" I asked.

"Best darn week of my whole life!" he exclaimed.

"You've got to be kidding," I said, incredulous.

"Made new friends from as far as Huntsville. Kissed a girl. Met Jesus by the lake night before last. I always thought I was a Christian—only religion I ever got to try. But here at camp, now I know I'm really a Christian. I'm different."

And all my hours languishing in board meetings, all my days of despair at the status of camp vanished. That young disciple reminded me of what a great treasure had been committed to my well-meaning but inept oversight. I was different.

I could feel it.

CHAPTER SEVEN

BISHOPS PREACHING

All God gives us Christian leaders to move people forward is nonviolent words. Transformative leaders help people live toward a new world by telling a story that is counter to the one that holds them captive. Jesus came preaching. Just as God said, "Let there be light" and there was (Gen. 1), so Jesus dismantles an old world and brings a new with nothing but words.

Shortly after my sermon at the National Cathedral—a faux rant against demagogue Glenn Beck (based on John 9), Fox News fired Beck. The next week my pastors gave me lists of people to terminate by mentioning their names in my sermons. Am I a great preacher or what?

As a new bishop I was thrilled to discover that I was already competent in the most important aspect of episcopal leadership: using words and stories to motivate and to persuade.[1] "Take thou authority to preach the word . . ." was the charge, so many years ago, when I was ordained. Bishops possess the same power enjoyed by all pastors—the noncoercive power to talk Christians into doing things they would not have attempted on their own.

One of my fears as a bishop was to wake up one day and find myself nothing but a sanctified CEO going to meetings, making decisions, shuffling papers. Therefore a bishop must pray, "Lord, keep me a United Methodist preacher." Fortunately, all I was ever called to be is what the church needs now from its bishops.

Those who say that the best preparation for being bishop is to have previously been a district superintendent are wrong. The management work of DSs on the ground is sui generis and should not be confused with leadership by bishops in the balcony. Because I had never helped appoint a pastor, I came to the job fresh, open, and ignorant. Weekly preaching the truth that few want to hear, coaxing a congregation into believing the outlandish idea that Jesus Christ is the answer to what ails the world is bishop boot camp.

LISTENING LIKE A BISHOP

"Bishops need to listen," many told me. My heart sank. When somebody's talking, I want it to be me. And yet, as reading is prerequisite for writing, preaching thrives by listening. The twenty-minutes-of-words-worth-saying on Sunday require a preacher who listens all week. Preachers spend years learning to listen to a biblical text honestly, critically, accurately, and humbly—precisely the skills required for episcopal listening.

Isolated behind so many insiders and clergy types, I devised a number of stratagems to hear something new: listening an hour or so every few weeks to a young adult who was not a Christian, asking a host preacher to set up a lunch with a small group of her best lay leaders rather than go to lunch with the professional staff, disciplining myself to spend as much time in conversation with young clergy as I did with the old guard on my Cabinet, listening to the sermons of every full-time pastor I appointed, reading e-mail two hours a day, and praying at least once a year for each pastor by name with a picture of the pastor in front of me.

"Our bishop needs to listen" usually means "Bishop, listen to *me*." Most people who have the bishop's ear want to talk about the protection of the status quo. The trick is to find people who have not been heard.

Scripture teaches that when God speaks it's usually through those who, before God summoned them, were marginalized and voiceless. More important than knowing how to listen is to know

114

to whom to listen. In my first days, eager to show that I was a good bishop, my door was open, so eager was I to talk to anyone, anytime, anyplace. Good decisions require good information. Trouble is, most of the people who wanted to talk, particularly in the days before they knew me, came with an agenda: here is work that I want to take off my back and lay on yours.

A hierarchical system deludes people into thinking that power flows from the top down. An anxious organization yearns for omnipotent saviors to fix it by executive fiat. In such a climate, lots of people think that the easiest way get a fix is to talk the bishop into their agenda and then wait for the bishop to get busy. Conversation with the bishop gives the illusion that they have actually accomplished something without expending much effort since now they've enlisted the bishop to do work that God meant for them.

When confronted by those who say, "God has given me a great idea that I want to lay on you," a bishop must say, "I am already working full-time. It appears that God has given you an assignment. God has said nothing of this to me. By all means, obey God's vocation and get busy. Let me know how it works out."

Productive people assume personal responsibility and are generally far too busy to waste time talking to the bishop. Thus, unless a bishop is selective, he or she will spend more time with those who are failing at ministry than with those who are succeeding—failing people feel better if they can explain their failure to you, hoping that you will take responsibility for their failure. These are the "I could succeed at ministry but the dumb Cabinet has never sent me to a good church" pastors.

Any group that begins planning by first attempting to get a number of bishops at the gathering probably doesn't know how to do the creative work required to produce a worthwhile meeting. I therefore routinely asked DSs, "Convene a half dozen of your most productive pastors and their lay leadership. I need to encourage them and to learn from them."

It's axiomatic that most of a good manager's time should be spent with the organization's best people. In a system in which two-thirds of the pastors and churches are failing to fulfill the full purpose of the church and its ministry, selective listening is essential.

During my first couple of months, I engaged in about twenty listening sessions with all of our clergy. In the first groups, the first questions concerned The UMC and homosexuality. Our church has a clear, legislated position on ordaining homosexual persons. What about "no" could they not understand?

"Can we be sure that you will support the *Discipline's* position on homosexuality?" they asked. I was insulted. I've vowed to administer the *Discipline*. They had just met me and already suspected that I was a liar?

"Our conference has lost a fourth of its membership in the last two decades. There has not been one instance of any confusion over where we stand on ordaining gay people. In your first two hours with your bishop, this is your greatest concern?"

Sometimes people talk about certain subjects because they are less threatening. A leader must find a way to get the institution talking about issues it has been avoiding for decades. So the challenge is not simply to listen, but also to refocus the conversation by asking the right questions. Writers connected with agitation groups like Renew Network, the Reconciling Movement, the Good News Movement, the IRD, Methodist Federation for Social Action, and the Confessing Movement sometimes say that they talk so much about sex because it's the cause of our decline. There is no evidence for any such claim. Their attempt to keep our church focused on sexuality is owing more to their fundraising than to the issue's theological importance.[2]

A leader refocuses a conversation by asking better questions: "Have you excluded gay and lesbian persons from your congregations?" If someone is openly gay in Alabama and still wants to follow Jesus as a United Methodist—even after the ugly things we've said about their particular brand of sin—"Don't we need them to teach the rest of us the art of forgiveness?"

Bishops, like anyone else with power to talk, need to hear the truth in order to utilize power with care. But powerful people often have power to do almost anything except to force people to tell us the truth.[3] Gregory the Great warns that a bishop, "by the very fact of his preeminence over others, becomes conceited; and because everything is at his service, because his orders are quickly executed to suit his wishes, because all his subjects praise him for what he has done well, but have no authority to criticize what he has done amiss . . . his mind, led astray by those below him, is lifted above itself . . . he is diverted by the commendations of others." The bishop thus becomes deluded into thinking, "himself to be wiser than any of those whom he exceeds in power."[4]

My first month on the job I said something mildly humorous and my Cabinet erupted in peals of laughter. I was terrified.[5]

Bishops have been removed for the sin of adultery, and well they should, but adultery is more easily avoided by a bishop than vanity. If surrounded by deferential, flattering sycophants, a bishop is sorely tempted to believe adulators and disregard detractors. If lying is the mother of vanity, arrogance is vanity's child.[6] Max Weber urged the cultivation of "distance toward oneself" as an antidote to vanity—a bishop needs "balcony time" not only from the demands of the organization but also from the demands of the ego.

Nan Keohane advises a leader to foster a "pragmatic realism" coupled with a "sardonic sense of humor."[7] I'm sure that Nan, my former boss, could testify I've got one of those virtues down pat. Humor, in all its forms, may be the supremely humanizing instance of "balcony time," a short vacation from having always to be right.

Dear reader, do not overly concern yourself about bishops bloated by vainglory and arrogance—the sheer magnitude of decline and failure in The UMC make depression and despair greater episcopal temptations.

Talking like a Bishop

We preachers tend toward loquaciousness. Any leader who is guardian of an organization's guiding purposes must be a big talker, relentlessly reiterating our core values. While the church is a frail, thoroughly human organization, it is not exclusively human. A bishop must reiterate our theological identity as the Body of Christ. The Trinity not only determines the purposes of the church but also provides our agency to fulfill those purposes. The Holy Spirit wants to ally with us. Patsy kidded that she could tell whenever I was urging the church to do some impossible task for which I anticipated tough resistance by how redundantly I referred to the second person of the Trinity in my speech: "Jesus wants us to . . . and Jesus expects us to . . . and we owe it to Jesus to . . ."

That's a major reason why I instituted the "Bishop's Weekly Message."[8] I average receiving about thirty e-mail responses to each week's message. One of my young clergy initiated a blog utilizing these messages.[9] Our conference director of communication (one of the most important conference positions) established a weekly podcast, replaying my sermons and lectures. Something like ten thousand people download those podcasts weekly. I also use Twitter and Facebook.

By the end of my first year, technology had enabled me to have extended conversations with more than two hundred of my clergy. Online correspondence enables a bishop to explain and to listen, to meet and to cultivate new, young clergy (who feel most comfortable with online communication) as well as to identify clergy in trouble. E-mail gives some people enough communicative rope to hang themselves, providing valuable insights for a bishop. Blogs are a great way for people to step up, speak out, and lead. When one of our retired clergy, a Republican member of the state legislature, attempted on our conference blog site to defend his vote for an ill-conceived immigration bill, his fellow clergy called him to account; I didn't have to.

Listening to my preachers' sermons, I learned that one of a preacher's greatest challenges is clarity. The laity complain that their preachers tackle too many subjects, wander down too many divergent paths, and are therefore difficult to follow. Good sermons are dependent on clarity about what a preacher will talk about and also ruthless lucidity about what one refuses to discuss. Thus Gregory the Great advises a bishop to "be discreet in keeping silence and profitable in speech, lest he utter what should be kept secret, or keep secret what should be uttered."[10]

A number of observers agree: healthy congregations have clarity about their corporate identity and can clearly communicate that identity to others.[11] From what I've seen, while vibrant congregations tend to be diverse in the identities of their members and draw on diverse sources for their vibrancy, they share an ability clearly to name who God means them to be and who they are not meant to be.

Before I became bishop, I interviewed a dozen bishops, about half of whom were retired. The majority said that the job is impossible. I learned that their gloomy view of the episcopacy said more about their inability to focus on the one essential thing than to the impossibility of the job.

Very soon a bishop must clarify the most important things to talk about. Clarity came when my conference added one little word to our Vision: "Every church challenged and equipped to grow *more* disciples . . ." Of all the things needed in my churches, hardly a church has any problems that couldn't be solved by having more people worshiping the Trinity. Growth became my relentless message. The Father loves to bring into being things that were not. The kingdom of God grows. The Holy Spirit expands anything it touches. Growth, growth, growth.

Thus the Call to Action of the Council of Bishops declares that we bishops must "refashion and strengthen our approaches in leadership development, deployment, and supervision. We must articulate dramatically higher performance expectations and commit to achieving them—with a much greater emphasis on outputs

119

as contrasted with intentions and activities."[12] The CTA calls for "greater clarity about outcomes" by instituting and reporting "measurable performance results in all sectors of the connection on an ongoing and regular basis."

The need for clarity of message also means that though stamping out malaria and eradicating killer diseases in Africa, fostering civility of speech in public discourse, limiting our carbon footprint, disposing of land mines, ending unjustified wars in the Near East—to name just a few of the assignments given to me in the past four years by earnest members of the COB—are worthy causes, they are not as important as the one thing needful right now, right here in Alabama. If these matters are to be brought to the attention of my conference, someone else must say it, not me. I'm the guy who talks growth.

Sad to say, it is easier to push the preposterous notion that our church is going to eradicate the world's killer diseases than to focus on the boredom that is killing our church.

One of my DSs asked every congregation to do just one thing: make one new Christian this year. Too small a goal? The DS pointed out that it's a goal unreached by over half of UM congregations. Small goals are important in declining institutions.[13] Shrink the change in order not to overwhelm with change.

I've always tended to tackle too many things at once. It's helpful to have people around me who remind me to stick with the few things that are essential and possible. All significant change requires a few victories to celebrate rather than to risk being overwhelmed with many defeats.

Good preaching talks about what God talks about, focuses on Scripture, and forms itself according to the patterns of Scripture. Through words, a bishop directs the church's attention by talking about matters that the church is more comfortable to keep silent on. We also retell our corporate story to enable the church to look through the lens of our master story—reiterating the story of what God has done in Jesus Christ to recover Creation.

Sadly, the more skilled the speaker, the more suspicious the constituency. (Some resent President Obama's skilled rhetoric.) There is among many Americans a populist tendency to respond positively to inarticulate people (i.e., Sarah Palin). Preachers have much experience persuading people through a diverse range of verbal appeals. Scripture is our model in its dizzying array of literary forms that bring to speech the truth who is Jesus Christ.

And besides, whether they listen or refuse to listen (Ezek. 2:5), acceptance of the message by the listeners has never been the supreme test of Christian communication. The majority of us are United Methodist by birth rather than through new commitment to the Wesleyan way of being Christian. Therefore our pastors are sometimes lulled into the false security of thinking that our people have already been formed into the faith. They feel free to preach on nonbiblical drivel such as purpose-driven lives, more meaningful existence, happier families, and well-adjusted sexuality. Though the CTA says that we need more "topical" and less "lectionary" preaching, I say, topical or lectionary, in a church in great need of the theological rationale for the church, what we need is more *biblical* preaching. Having more new and prospective Christians among our listeners could cure much of what's wrong with our preaching. (Growth!) Until that happens, we ought to go back over the key narratives of the faith, reforming our people into the peculiar purposes of the church within the Wesleyan tradition. Our most insightful pastors are recovering from the now dated, Constantinian assumption that the North American church lives in a basically Christian culture, where the culture is a helpful prop for the church. That United Methodists now find ourselves increasingly feeling like aliens in the culture we thought we once owned is a grand call for a refurbishment of the teaching office of the episcopacy.

I averaged publishing at least one book a year[14] and conducted conference-wide teaching sessions on Christians and War, the Wesleyan Way of Believing, use of *The Wesley Study Bible*, immigration legislation, racism and the Christian faith, as well as my yearly class on Jesus at Birmingham-Southern College.

As Gil Rendle said, "We tend to know more about who we *were* than who we *are*."[15] I worry that when the COB begins its spring meeting with a memorial service, focusing on those who once were bishops, it tends to distract us from the awesome responsibilities of those who currently are bishops. Thus I accepted few invitations to celebrate a congregation's centenary but moved heaven and earth to be with my (relatively few) congregations that showed they wanted to work with Jesus into the future. Having a vital present and a hopeful future begins in reiteration of the theological fact that the church exists, not for itself, but rather to save the world. And how do we fulfill that absurdly expansive task? By proclaiming in word and deed the advent of a new world, proclaiming "the mighty acts of him who called you out of darkness into his marvelous light" (1 Peter 2:9). Now.

Much of the learning that is required is *un*learning. People function as they have been taught and produce the results that they have learned to produce. When the Cabinet and I removed a pastor after noticing the decline in attendance and the few baptisms in his first six months at a church, I received an angry call from a layperson. "What are you doing to us? That pastor is helping us heal after our past conflict."

Through the inspiration of the Holy Spirit, I said to him, "I hear you are a successful businessperson. Look at your church's past six months on our conference Dashboard. If you hired an employee and he produced those same numbers in his first six months, would you not conclude that the employee, for any of his good intentions, would not find a way to be productive?"

"I didn't know that we were allowed to ask that sort of question about our clergy," said the man. That evening telephone conversation was my best lecture on ecclesiology.

"Organizational adaptation occurs through experimentation," according to Heifetz, Grashow, and Linsky.[16] A spirit of experimentation is more needed than one of care, caution, and planning. We cannot modify our systemic failure without the encouragement of experiments, well-intentioned failures, and learning from failures.

We worked for two years to produce a perfect residency in ministry program for new provisional clergy to give them what they had missed in seminary. The program functioned barely one year until the money gave out and all those perfect plans were jettisoned in favor of a year-to-year, streamlined, more flexible effort. Over-planning is often the result of an over-cautious ethos that is afraid to fail.

Christian repentance-forgiveness ought to be a resource to leaders in church experimentation: "Hey, let's try it and see what happens. If God refuses to bless our efforts and it fails, we will kill it and try something else without feeling guilty."

Methodist clergy were once primarily referred to as "preachers." We took a wrong turn in the last century when we started calling ourselves "pastors." Caregiving to the congregation rather than proclamation of the gospel became our primary duty. Our ministry became judged by how well we nursed our flock rather than by the congregation's ministry in the world. It's not only that pastoral care is too modest a vision for Christian leadership; it's also that a primary way we care is through clear articulation of the faith. A greater challenge than to create a warm relationship with fellow Christians is to be obedient to the Trinity. That's why good preachers are always great risk-takers who have a nearly weekly experience of failure. A bishop must model risk taking for risk-averse pastors.

MAKING GOOD DECISIONS

A static, closely managed system attempts to keep a lid on information. A retired DS told me that when he served on the Cabinet the most frequently heard phrase was, "I remind you of our commitment to confidentiality. Nothing gets outside this room, and do not discuss anything related to pastoral appointments away from this table."

Confidentiality becomes a big concern for leaders who value control more than good results and are unable to give rational explanations for the decisions they make. In communication, we share power, enlisting the help—and sometimes the pointed criticism—of stakeholders in the decision. My watchword to the Cabinet was, "Talk, talk among yourselves, talk to everyone you meet about the challenges of deploying our clergy for the mission of the church. Let people know that you're always thinking about the best utilization of our best people, and listen, listen to one another, listen to rumors, answer all correspondence, even the letters from 'Anonymous.' "

What looks like pushback is often a simple lack of clarity, a request for more information rather than ossified resistance.

A bishop's key organizational function is to make the right decisions for the good of the church, and good decisions are a function of good communication.[17] Mickey Connolly and Richard Rianosher in *The Communication Catalyst*[18] identify four ways of making decisions that foster either change or deadlock.

Authoritative decision-making puts decisions in the hands of someone with authority. Everyone else stops thinking and worries about following the authority's rules. Maybe there was a day when bishops worked like this.

Voting gives away authority to the majority and nobody takes responsibility for a decision. After the vote, those who lose are alienated. The contributions of experts are ignored as nonexperts determine the decision. Ah, the picture of General Conference grows clearer!

Consensus demands that everyone deliberates and all agree, a process that takes huge amounts of time, even though consensus is usually an unrealistic expectation when a group is faced with really difficult decisions. Consensus leadership sacrifices creativity for conformity and tends to alienate those who refuse to go along to get along. Many pastors I know are paralyzed by their fantasy that there is some way to lead the Body of Christ by achieving consensus among all members. The oft-heard slogan in

The UMC "We need everyone's voice at the table" is a sure sign that the process of discussion is more important than a good decision.

Contributive decisions harness the intelligence of the group to make quick, valuable decisions where expertise is connected to risk and people are invited to have a stake in the decision. This is how I wanted to work as a bishop. In contributive decisions a leader must see the big picture and be willing to be answerable for the consequences of the decision. Voices are sought who are able to give input about feasibility and consequences. External coaches and advisors are sometimes called in to offer expert advice. Recipients are informed of the decision and are kept posted as the organization lives into the decisions. If the decision leads to bad consequences, mistakes are admitted and contributors are sought to help fix the problem.

Constant, clear communication is the primary way to work through resistance and conflict due to the challenge of change. As a preacher, I am required to attempt to love my congregation as Jesus loves them, sacrificing some of my self-regard in order to be worthy of the privilege of preaching the way, the truth, and the life. Jesus' command to love our neighbor is most difficult when my neighbor and I have a difference of opinion. But Jesus' neighbor love was a command, not a suggestion. Furthermore, it would have been challenge enough to be commanded by Jesus to love my neighbor, but Jesus commanded me to love my *enemy*. A bishop without enemies is a bishop who is failing to show up for work.

A retired clergyman, who had been a DS some years ago, fiercely opposed some of the changes I was attempting to lead. His reaction seemed to me over-the-top. In the middle of his enumeration of the reasons I was a disaster, he said, "I once worked hand-in-hand with the bishop."

For the first time God enabled me really to hear this brother's plea—I have lost my status. I was on my way to loving my neighbor as myself. In conflict, search for areas of agreement. Lead with positive questions like, "What do you like about our plan to reorganize the conference?" Listening is not passive. I must listen with compassion (Latin, "to suffer with"): asking questions in order to understand, assuming that, as yet, I have not understood what is bothering this person, not interrupting, listening for possibility of agreement.

I learned from Bishops James King and Larry Goodpaster to ask, "Could you say more?" It's a way to buy time to think and also to signal a desire to better understand. Among people's greatest needs—along with food, sex, and safety—is a desire to be heard. If I keep asking the right questions, they will find a way to tell the truth, often truth I have been avoiding. Because of baptism, I've got to assume that my conversation partner—for all his prickly, low remarks about me—is a brother in Christ whose desire to be faithful to the mission of Jesus may exceed my own.

Clarity is close cousin of simplicity. The Heaths tell business leaders, "If you say three things, you don't say anything,"[19] thus demolishing the old "three-points-and-a-poem" sermon model. Relentless communication, continuous repetition, and constant clarity are requisites for transformative leadership. My sixth-grade math teacher could tell you that I've got the sort of mind that is prone to wander, is interested in everything, and quickly loses interest in a problem once I've figured it out for myself. I don't like having to go back through my own laborious journey toward a solution in order to invite others to walk the same path.

And yet, that is just what interesting preachers do—preach in a way that invites the congregation to go on the same journey that has led to the insights in the sermon.

Ken Blanchard said that change must be orchestrated, utilizing all kinds of media, and that an idea needs to be communicated at least seven times, seven different ways, before the idea is received by the constituency.[20] My academic background was a liability for this sort of communication. Academics distrust simplicity; the scholar's job is to put as many possible explanations on the table for allegedly open consideration. I'm in good company on my academically induced turgidity—critics cite murky communication and conflicting messages as a major contributor to Rowan Williams's episcopal misery.[21]

In the early days of my episcopacy I was criticized by the Episcopacy Committee for talking too harshly and by the Cabinet for talking too much. Guilty. I tend to think with my mouth open. When I put some idea before the Cabinet for consideration, a DS responded, "Let's hear this week's brilliant idea."

A leader's lack of clarity and simplicity in message, a failure to focus on the absolutely essential work that could make a difference, leads to ideas that don't stick.[22]

Some of my many ideas that didn't stick:

- Let's have Communion on Sundays when I visit a congregation.
- Let's do away with district offices and have DSs work out of their cars while constantly on the road.
- Send your young, talented lay leadership to annual conference.
- Let's do away with our entire connectional ministries staff and wait and see which functions the churches demand we reinstitute.
- Let's close any church that refuses to participate in any way in our connectional giving program.
- Let's start a new church with only lay leadership that never acquires real estate.
- Let's not have our usual annual conference and instead confess that we are not sure of what we are doing, are unhappy about our results, and then spend two days in prayer and discernment.

Ideas that stuck were those that many people had had before I enunciated them. Truly original ideas rarely stick. We must listen for ideas that come with, "I've always said that someday we ought to . . ." And we must listen in order to discover those people who not only have novel ideas but also are willing to take responsibility and say, "Bishop, give me permission and I'll show you how to do this."

To be honest, what The United Methodist Church needs now are not more good ideas but more insights for what we ought to do next. Our lack is decisiveness, courage, agency, someone to say, "Let's endure the pain in order to give our church a future." Bishops may be among the few persons in The UMC who are willing to decide that our church ought to have a future. However, decisiveness is dependent on first achieving clarity and focus.

Sadly, the propensity of the COB as well as General Conference to lay a host of vision pathways, goals, quadrennial emphases, and slogans on us has the effect of diffusing our message and deflecting our energies. It isn't that our church is doing too little, it is rather that we are attempting to do too much in too many places and our busyness is robbing us of our ability to do the things most needful at this particular time and place.

Like preaching, leadership is a performance. Every day a bishop, like any pastor, is forced by the needs of the church and the call of God to act like a spiritual leader even when he or she doesn't feel like it, even when, by want of character or inclination, he or she is personally not that well suited to the demands of the role.

Like preaching, leadership is more easily learned than taught, requiring a complex of skills that are in short supply among humanity. Even as preachers require listeners to make preaching work, leaders require followers. There are a number of essential prerequisites for the job of bishop—personal experience of the constantly transforming and renewing grace of God in Jesus Christ, a good liberal arts education followed by a classical seminary education, personal experience feeding from the fleshpots of Egypt, years of pastoral experience in a variety of church contexts, a high IQ, great empathy with other human beings, administrative expertise, a resonate voice, a humble and contrite spirit, and deep knowledge of the Scriptures. Failing personally to have all of those gifts, like any preacher, a bishop at least ought to be called. Most days, thank God, this is enough.

CHAPTER EIGHT

BISHOPS TEACHING

Jesus, the Good Shepherd, attempted a respite from the press of ministry and withdraws to a "deserted place" (Mark 6:30 ff.). But once Jesus and his disciples arrive at the desert, it is anything but deserted. Teeming multitudes press on him. Jesus has "compassion" because they are "like sheep without a shepherd." Faced with such vast human need, what does Jesus do?

He teaches. He will give them bread, but not before he gives them the Word. Among all the needs among these shepherdless sheep, Jesus gives priority to teaching.

A historic function of bishops, shepherd of the shepherds under the Good Shepherd, is teaching, guarding, and transmitting the faith. Teaching not only helps a church stay close to its purpose by reiterating to the church its odd identity, teaching helps a church adapt discipleship in our time and place. Wesley embodied this pedagogical function with gusto, publishing scores of pamphlets and books, making Methodism a large, far-flung classroom. Peculiar practices like connectionalism and itinerancy do not come naturally; Methodists had to be taught. The first American bishops, Coke and Asbury, connected this frontier faith movement through education. By the Civil War, Methodists had founded nearly two hundred schools and colleges as well as several publishing houses. Teaching was one of the few episcopal practices in which I had much experience, so my own episcopacy was one of teaching.[1]

Gil Rendle, utilizing the insights of Ron Heifetz, noted that in order to renew itself, The United Methodist Church has been engaging in mostly "technical work." Technical work Heifetz defined as the search for the right application of technique to solve known problems—our earlier application of the insights of the church growth movement (which I eagerly and rather naively applied to my inner-city parish in the early 1980s), congregational transformation (those workshops that I led in churches during the late 1980s), and leadership development (district seminars helping clergy retool their skills to lead in the 1990s).[2] For all the good in these efforts, as Gil said laconically, "they didn't get us all the way to where we wanted to go."[3]

ADAPTIVE LEADERSHIP

More than problem solving and platitudes, we needed conversion of beliefs and assumptions. I love technical work because it focuses upon action. But now—if what was needed was a change of beliefs and assumptions—more than a commander, I needed to be a more curious learner, a constant questioner, and a creative teacher. That's what Heifetz calls "adaptive work"—helping an organization adapt to its environment on the basis of its purposes and values by facing the painful realities and then mobilizing new attitudes and behaviors.[4] Leaders get attention, focus attention, frame issues, and orchestrate conflict[5] in the hope that people will see the opportunity and embrace the challenge. Adaptive change is deep change because it aims at the modification of an organization's culture rather than discarding a few of its practices.[6]

Before asking, "What should we do?" adaptive leadership poses questions of *identity*—"Who are we?" and questions of *purpose*—"Why are we here?" and *goals*—"Where are we being called to go?" I often wish that I made changes sooner, but Heifetz counsels, "Resist the leap into action." Spend time in analysis and interpretation.[7]

Adaptive work requires an educator, more specifically. a storyteller. (A *preacher!*) We can act only within the world in which we live and we can live only in a world we can see and we can see only the world we can speak. Stories create world. The one who would change people must offer better stories. The old story, "We are United Methodist—the biggest, most vibrant, most progressive denomination in the land," must be replaced by a story that begins, "God has given us all that we need to thrive into the future if we utilize the grace and the courage to tell the truth about ourselves and then to figure out which God-given talents are most needed to live out the truth of Jesus Christ in our time and place."

Adaptive leadership works the gap between people's expressed, shared values and the reality of their lives.[8] Not long ago, bishops who tried to fit into the operative story in our church were frustrated by the futility of attempting to work a story that no longer made sense. An adaptive, transformative leader takes the story that is there and attempts to retrieve and emphasize certain neglected aspects, reframing it as a more adequate story for the future. Thus I loved preaching in my churches on Martin Luther King Weekend when I could reclaim the story of Methodism in Alabama—stories of Methodists who did the right thing (and those who didn't)—and preach these stories from our past in order to narrate us into the future.

A frequent charge against unproductive UM clergy is that they are "lazy"; a too-simple explanation for clerical exhaustion due to unfocused ministry,[9] clergy rushing about doing everything in an attempt to live out a now inadequate story of ministry.

In their book, *The Practice of Adaptive Leadership*, Heifetz and Linsky characterized adaptive change in these ways:[10]

- *Adaptive leadership is about change that enables the capacity to thrive.*

I repeatedly announced that decline was not our fate and that I had faith that we could grow if we were willing to take an honest look at ourselves and, by God's grace, adapt ourselves to the mission of Christ.

131

- *Successful adaptive changes build on the past rather than jettison it.*

I delayed making changes in the Cabinet, thinking it important to try to talk these key, traditional leaders into stepping into a new story before I attempted to change anyone else. Appealing to core characteristics of our conference history—such as our ability to change during the 1960s—I affirmed that core as who we really are and wanted again to be.

- *Organizational adaptation occurs through experimentation.*

Urging people not to worry about setting long-term precedents, I noticed and rewarded experimenters, promising that we would evaluate the experiments and toss aside what didn't work—without guilt—attempting to identify people who had God-given gifts for innovation and experimentation and to replace people who stressed continuity and predictability.

- *Adaptation relies on diversity.*

I brought more people into the conversation and delighted in discovering someone who had not previously been a leader in our church stepping up and taking responsibility. I encouraged experiments to occur simultaneously, inviting as many new ideas as possible, allowing better ideas to replace ineffective ideas. My conference is not a battleship; it's a flotilla of diverse boats. Bishops must love diversity, marvel at the rich array of gifts God has given the church, and eschew bureaucratic uniformity.

- *New adaptations significantly displace, reregulate, and rearrange some old DNA.*

Attempting to get as many people on board as possible, we rotated people on and off the Cabinet after short terms, ignored ineffective structures, and fostered a culture of "This is what we are doing now, but we serve a living God so we may strike our tents and move elsewhere next year."

- *Adaptation takes time.*

God has not seen fit to give me a surfeit of patience. And yet God takes time. Grace is not grace if it's predictable or programmed. God waited over four hundred years before rescuing Israel from Egyptian slavery. For reasons known only to God, God blesses some of our efforts and refuses to bless others. It took me six years to feel effective. Thus I prayed, "Lord, make me more patient, now!"

A bishop's power is akin to the power of pastors, leaders whose leadership is, in great part, a gift bestowed upon them by the congregation. Nan Keohane said, "We follow because leaders sometimes show us possibilities for action or improvement beyond anything we might have envisioned."[11]

A retired bishop whom I greatly admire, particularly for his prophetic commitment to the marginalized, was noted for his prophetic voice, but not for his prophetic action. A layperson commented, "He is full of good Christian values and noble intentions. He couldn't put his holy precepts into mundane practice. He just never touched down on earth anywhere. We admired him but couldn't figure out how to follow him."

I did so much preaching in congregations in my conference because I quickly surmised that the church had little desire for a bishop who was a sanctified CEO. Episcopal bishops are fortunate to be expected to perform the confirmations in the diocese. Liturgical leadership designates the episcopal bishop as a leader of a particular species. While I sought out opportunities to confirm new Christians and begged to be allowed to lead the Eucharist when I visited a congregation, as a UM bishop, preaching contextualized me, identified me as more than a servant of the organization; I am a "servant of the Word," Luther's favorite designation for clergy. Preaching also demonstrated that I was attached to a higher standard than the church's adulation or scorn.

The limitation of the input of bishops solely to an occasional sermon and to the episcopal address is only one of the dysfunctions of General Conference. We have a great need for bishops to reassume their primary historic role as teachers of the church, as God gives us the gifts. An effective leader floods the system with information in the faith that the system has the resources to respond.

Heifetz distinguishes between leadership that means merely manipulating "the community to follow the leaders' vision" and leadership that influences "the community to face its problems."[12] John Kotter highlights the transformative nature of leadership by distinguishing between managers and leaders: "management is about coping with complexity," while "leadership is about coping with change."[13] Social progress requires leaders who are willing to risk disapproval and even rejection in the interest of transformation.

Matthew's Gospel ends with the risen Christ appearing before his disciples. Some of his disciples worshiped; others doubted. What did they doubt? The risen Christ stood in front of them, had been with them for weeks. Surely they didn't doubt that he was resurrected.

Christ says, "All authority in heaven and on earth has been given to me." Authority to do what? Authority to commission. "Go, therefore, into all the world and make disciples, baptizing and teaching all that I have commanded you."

That must be why "some doubted." Some doubted Jesus' authority, or at least his good judgment, in commissioning this rag-tag group of losers to be the ones to "Go . . . make disciples . . . baptizing . . . teaching . . ." Episcopal leadership rests upon faith, faith in Jesus that overcomes our doubts in ourselves.

In my early listening sessions with clergy, I asked, "What do you most need from your new bishop?" I recorded their responses and devised a list of their expressed leadership needs that I wanted to fulfill: *We want a bishop who listens, but who then can make timely decisions. We want a bishop to be a person who is formed by Scripture. Our new bishop really needs to convince us that we should change and we can change. You've got to do something about ineffective clergy. A good preacher. I want a bishop who knows me, really knows me, and then places me where I can best serve the church. Just once I would like to see the bishop and Cabinet surprise us; our clergy appointments are so boringly predictable. Find a way to let the people of Alabama know that there is more than one kind of Christian in our state. I wish our bishop would hang out with someone other than just our eldest clergy.*

Then I prayerfully made a list of their expectations that, with God's help, I had no intention of fulfilling: *We want a bishop who spends more time just hanging out with us and getting to know us and our families. A bishop has got to have his hand on everything that goes on in our conference. You ought to be in your office at least three days a week. When appointments are being made, you need to give more attention to the needs of our spouses and our families. Bishops should attend more meetings of the connectional ministries team. We need you to exercise more leadership in the general church agencies and boards. It is not too much to expect our bishop to be at the yearly meetings of United Methodist Women. You should honor the years of faithful service that some of us have put into the church and insure our upward professional advancement. Reorganize United Methodist Men. Appoint more African American pastors to salaries of over sixty-thousand dollars.*

The five characteristics of adaptive organizations are:

1. Elephants in the room are named.
2. Responsibility for the organization's future is shared.
3. Independent judgment is expected.
4. Leadership capacity is developed.
5. Reflection and continuous learning is institutionalized.[14]

Heifetz believes that the qualities of an intellectual—the willingness to learn, to grow, to be surprised, to notice specific differences and variations, and to adapt—are essential attributes for effective leaders. Being bishop was my most intellectually demanding role in years.[15] After more than twenty years in academia, I found it intellectually invigorating to have a job where I was overwhelmed, had to ask for help, was forced to read books on business and management that I wouldn't have touched if I had had my own way, and scrambled every day to spend time with someone who had a new idea. Leadership is more than finding power and exercising authority; leadership is an educational practice.

The past is a leader's greatest competitor, said Max Weber, "the authority of the eternal yesterday,"[16] the holiness of habit and the comfort of conformity. The recognition that "our world is no longer the way it was" provokes questions: "How have I benefited from, and felt comfortable in, the old world?" "How am I threatened by the world that now is?" "What skills would I need better to live in the new world?"

Walter Brueggemann told a group of us clergy, "If you won't let God use you to make a new world, then all you can do is to service the demands of the old world and that's no fun."

Bishops have tended to confuse leadership with authority, power, and influence perhaps because the church gives bishops considerable power and some authority. Thanks be to God that ministry is never a solo act. God gives us people with gifts to help us do work that we cannot, and God graciously puts us in situations in which we must reach out for help or else appear incredibly arrogant in our attempts at self-sufficiency. I got a management coach and I met periodically with a small group of United Methodist businesspersons because I knew I needed help with systemic analysis and structural change. Even Jesus looked upon the hungry, hurting multitudes and responded to their need, not with "I had better get busy proving to them that I'm the all-sufficient Savior of the world," but rather with, "Everybody pray that the Lord will send us enough workers to handle the harvest" (Matt. 9:38 author version).[17]

I noticed that I got better questions and insights when I led meetings where both clergy and laypersons were present rather than just clergy. The laity, perhaps because in their daily work they were more experienced in organizational change and adaptation, seemed more supportive of new measures in accountability and innovation. Or perhaps they had less at stake than the clergy in the preservation of the old world.

SICK SYSTEMS?

Heifetz spoke of "the illusion of a broken system"[18] in which a leader says, "This thing is broken; let's fix it." The appointive process? Broken. The itinerancy? Sick unto death. The COB? Dysfunctional. Seminaries? Unproductive.

A system works the way that key people in the system want it to work. For instance, I have criticized the World Methodist Council for not producing anything worth the cost of its expensive meetings. "We spend most of our meetings," reports a friend on the WMC, "discussing 'Why are we here?' "

Then someone suggested to me that the purpose of the WMC is to have a meeting, to enable once-prominent evangelical leaders of our church to have a forum for their voices, and to get as many people as possible to come from as many places as possible to the meeting. The WMC was created to be a sort of United Nations for The United Methodist Church. Fine. Rather than attempt to make the WMC "functional," The UMC ought to ask itself, "Ought we finance a group that has these functions?"

"Systems produce what they are designed to produce, and the current United Methodist system is designed to produce fewer congregations and fewer members," said Lyle Schaller.[19]

Instead of scapegoating pastors for our system's inability to grow, we ought to recognize the ways in which our system is well designed to produce certain results. The outcomes are those that were affirmed in another time and place but today, when we long for other outcomes, seem dysfunctional and sick. For instance, most congregations aspire for peace and inner congregational tranquility. Bishops and DSs have long evaluated a pastor's success on the pastor's ability always to heal divisions and preserve congregational peace. "Healing" was usually defined as an absence of conflict rather than a healthy ability to produce more disciples.

I have now expanded my definition of a "healthy church." The debate ought not to be who is to blame for producing the current outcomes but rather is it possible or even desirable for a bishop to aim for different outcomes?

For instance, I repeatedly urged my episcopal colleagues to reform our jurisdictional conference. Four days of laborious balloting to elect a few bishops, hours wasted waiting for ballots to be counted, filling time with pointless reports, sweating like dogs at Lake Junaluska. The last jurisdictional conference voted unanimously (upon a motion from North Alabama) to cut at least a day off the conference and to make the balloting more efficient. For the next two years, every time our jurisdictional college met, I pled with the bishops to fulfill the mandate and shorten and streamline the conference. A committee met repeatedly and each time reported, "There's no way we can shorten or make more efficient this meeting. This is the way we have to do it."

One of my fellow bishops said, "I expect that you are getting resistance to the change because you don't understand how much some people enjoy things just the way they are."

"But it is absurd to sit there for four days as bishops drone on and on about bishops when the whole point is to elect new bishops as quickly as possible and head for home."

"So you really think that's what bishops do at jurisdictional conference?" asked one of my colleagues after the meeting. "If you watch the jurisdictional conference work, I would say that you are watching bishops enjoy being bishops, enjoy some semblance of authority and adulation as they sit upon the stage and oversee the sweating multitude seated on the floor, as bishops eulogize departed bishops and congratulate and praise retiring bishops and marvel at the wonder that this seething multitude once voted for them. We leave jurisdictional conference exhausted from the endless balloting and with the illusion that we have actually done important work. You are asking the wrong people to change jurisdictional conference."

So many of my inherited truths had to be revised or jettisoned by me in my first year as bishop: *Bishops need to be pastors to their pastors. Bishops get the big head when they are elected; they need to be one of us. Bishops ought to put more pastors in cross-racial appointments.* Many of these slogans had to be reframed, reviewed, and renegotiated as I adapted my previous worldview to the realities of being a transforming leader of a declining organization. Inherited wisdom must be transformed into guiding principles such as: *Bishops need to insure that all their pastors have the opportunity to receive emotional, physical support for the rigors of ministry. Bishops must realize that the church has called them to a particular sort of ministry where they must occupy the "balcony" and be responsible for a more panoramic view of the church. Bishops must strive for a racially inclusive church by strategically placing pastors who have gifts for producing racially inclusive congregations. Bishops must be certain that they are utilizing to the fullest the God-given gifts of all clergy—regardless of race, gender, or age—in leading the mission of each congregation. Producing more UM women and more ethnic minority UMs are worthier goals than larger pastoral salaries.*

Effective intervention and painful prioritizing followed by courageous action are the tasks that we still have left to do after we have done the essential adaptive work. Heifetz encourages leaders to fall in love with tough decisions—especially challenging in an organization with a culture of niceness, that is, a culture of avoidance of painful conversations. The leader has got to enjoy wading into situations in which values and worldviews collide. Once again, that a bishop is a preacher is a great help to being an adaptive leader.

"Don't even attempt to make anybody happy," a retired bishop advised. "The first year you make appointments, you will make a good many people happy, but you are bound to make at least 20 percent of the clergy and laity unhappy. Next year you produce unhappiness in 20 percent more. Do the math. In a mere five years you have, through your decisions, made everyone very unhappy at least once." That bishop helped me reframe my assumptive world so that producing happiness—rather than, say, effectiveness or faithfulness—was never my goal.[20]

Information collection and arrangement is a prelude to most good decisions. But then, once the information is in, someone (like a bishop) has got to make a decision or the whole body suffers. The modern world keeps telling itself that we are unable to decide because we just don't have enough information (bring in the computers) or we just haven't heard from enough people (have more meetings). In reality what we lack is creativity and courage.

Our conference Dashboard was a wonderful instrument. But that's all it was—a tool. It is easier to get eight hundred churches reporting every week than for eight DSs to make one painful decision on the basis of the information shown on the Dashboard.

Wherever there is the possibility of change, there is the possibility of conflict and wherever there is conflict there is need for a safe, structured environment where there's enough conflict to get energy going but without overwhelming the organization. Conflict must be orchestrated (the presiding function of bishops is not just at the meetings of the annual conference), and the bishop is sometimes the director of a discordant symphony. Attempting to eliminate or to neutralize conflict robs an organization of the energy that often makes conflict our great ally in change. Adaptive leadership brings to the surface and then orchestrates conflict for the sake of learning and change.

When Alabama passed the most poorly written immigration legislation in the country in 2011, my first impulse was to issue a condemnation. Fortunately, some of our talented young clergy composed a letter to the governor, got their fellow clergy to sign the letter, and led a series of conversations around the conference—all without the bishop forcing it upon them.

LEARNING TO BE A BISHOP

The morning of my election, as I was led from the gathered jurisdictional conference to the stage where the bishops sat, Bishop Marion Edwards leaned over to me and said, "Friend, you have just deepened your prayer life."

This job has driven me, time and again, to confess my ineptitude and ignorance, my inability to impact something that needed changing, and in great desperation, forced me to seek resources to enable me to do this work. I didn't fail that often in my previous position; for a bishop, failure is a nearly hourly occurrence. Prayer is necessary.

Learning requires reflection. In the tug and pull of managing the church, in the barrage of crises and hours of meetings, it is all too easy for a bishop to be caught up in the activity of the job without reflecting on the direction and purpose of the job. Heifetz lists "seven practical suggestions for bearing the responsibility that comes from leadership":

1. get on the balcony
2. distinguish self from role
3. externalize the conflict
4. use partners
5. listen, using oneself as data, practice self-reflection, find the means to invite outsiders' points of view
6. find a sanctuary, a place where you can hear yourself think
7. preserve a sense of purpose that is constantly defined and reiterated

Note that all seven of these practices are reflective and educational in purpose, insuring that the leader is a constant learner.

I learned to give thanks to God that my primary previous ministry leadership experience was in campus ministry. Campus ministry gives a pastor so many opportunities for failure. (How well I remember the time we blitzed the campus—after months of planning and a large expenditure of funds—inviting students to a weeklong forum on "Faith and Sexuality." First night, three students showed up.)

Thus when a pastor said to me, "Bishop, I know you are disappointed by the lousy turnout tonight. I thought we would have more people interested in hearing you speak."

I replied, "Have you forgotten that I spent twenty years in campus ministry? I know how to fail!"

The conventional wisdom, "Always put your most successful pastors on your Cabinet," may be the way to insure that you will surround yourself with uneducable people. "Successful pastors" sometimes have so few failures that they are fearful to ask, "Is there a better way to do this work?"

I conducted an experiment in prayer, writing a dozen of my pastors each week, telling them that I planned to focus on them by name in prayer in the next week, asking them for what they would like me to pray. I discovered new dimensions of prayer, and my pastors discovered new leadership from their bishop.

When a pastor protested being sent to an inner-city congregation and said, "I'm basically a suburban person who finds it difficult to relate to disadvantaged people," what joy to be able to say (after I cooled down a bit), "Look, I knew next to nothing about how to be a bishop in Alabama. I'm giving you the grand opportunity to grow in grace." A bishop leads not only in the ministry of teaching but also in the ministry of learning. The UMC itinerancy requires people who enjoy the challenge of reinventing themselves, having to acquire a new set of ministerial skills in service in a new ministerial context, and asking God for the grace to start all over again. Therefore, it is important for a bishop to model for the pastors how to ask for help, and how to seek criticism and feedback, and to show how to grow in service to the church.

CHAPTER NINE

BISHOPS IN COUNCIL

Don't like bishops. Fishy lot. Blessed are the meek, my foot!
They're all on the climb. Ever heard of meekness stopping a
bishop from becoming a bishop? Nor have I.
—Oxford professor of classics, Maurice Bowra, while
lunching at the Reform Club seated near a bishop.[1]

W henever I bring pastors onto the Cabinet, I tell them, "The job of a DS is bifocal—you must care for the pastors and churches of a district; you must also be a member of a team." The episcopacy is similarly collegial. I have never heard anyone speak positively of the Council of Bishops. Much of the criticism of the council is unfair, and many of the expectations are unrealistic; much of the dysfunction within the COB is addressed by the Call to Action. My good news is that after eight years on the Council I can confidently say that most of what urgently needs doing in our church has nothing to do with the action or inaction of the COB. One of the greatest recent moves of the COB is to state "making disciples" as the goal of the church and, as everybody knows, bishops do next to nothing to make disciples—Jesus reserves his best work for the arena of the local church.

While there are those who decry the bishops' focus on the local congregation, seeing this as a betrayal of UM connectionalism, I welcome renewed emphasis upon what God actually accomplishes at the grassroots. When "connection" is defined bureaucratically, as something produced through apportionments and boards and agencies, we have suffered. I think it's rather

143

remarkable that the bishops reaffirmed that the local church is the region of the Holy Spirit, the anvil upon which disciples are made, and where Jesus Christ is preached to the world and is followed by his people.

Perhaps now that bishops are focusing on the local church and testing our effectiveness by what happens there, the COB can stop wasting so much time attempting to speak to the whole world and discipline ourselves to speak to our people in congregation. If Obama (like Bush before him) couldn't find time to meet with the COB while we were convened in Washington, at least we could convene United Methodists and talk to them.

Russ Richey praised a "growing sense of episcopal agency" in the COB in which, beginning with a series of pastoral letters, "for the first time in almost two hundred years, the bishops in united fashion gave theological leadership to the church."[2] I guess. My prejudice is that our pastoral letters are the council at its most nostalgic and distracted. I praise the COB for being a sometimes worthwhile colloquium for collegial support and encouragement, training and equipment for leadership, and mutual accountability. Few of us bishops have had training to do the pressing, transformative work that the church needs from us. We have not been successful in theological reflection, though it's badly needed in our church. Usually, when the bishops attempt theology in our occasional pronouncements or as we debate some dilemma, it is a reminder of the diverse theologies that made us bishops. One reason our General Conference episcopal address is usually an innocuous mix of this and that is that our attempts to speak with one voice suggest that *United* Methodist Church is a misnomer.

From what I've seen, the theological divergences within the COB are not more numerous than the theological stances among the pastors and the churches of my conference. The church should expect us bishops to participate in the COB, sometimes put our theological differences on the table, point out the inconsistencies and biblical and doctrinal inadequacies in one another's point of view, and fight it out—then celebrate Eucharist together.

144

Some of the COB's pompous, theologically impertinent statements arise from our failure to note and to embrace our changed social context. There may have been a day when Methodist bishops felt some sort of sacred responsibility to make America work, to speak to every social issue, to snuggle up to the U.S. Congress, and to celebrate a bishop's picture on the cover of *Time*. That Constantinian arrangement is no more. The last and most expensive relic of that age is General Conference, a Methodist U.S. Congress. While we were sleeping, American popular culture moved away from 1950's liberal, civil religion, and our church shrank to the margins of American religious life, making a quadrennial, expensive, two-week talk-a-thon silly. Reading the excellent biography of Bishop Oxnam[3] confirms that UM bishops now live in an utterly changed world and lead a church that must better adapt to its now disestablished context. Lamenting that William McKinley was the last Methodist in the White House until George W. Bush, Russ Richey concludes his *History* by celebrating Hillary Clinton at General Conference, the closest we have come to real political power in recent years. Rather sad.

Don't worry about political radicalism in the COB's public political statements. A greater temptation is insipid romanticism. The COB continues to address the president, congress, and Americans on various political subjects where UM bishops have no impact—it is easier to tell the president what to do than to advise the church on how to thrive.

What a great opportunity to rediscover the unique, countercultural integrity of being the Body of Christ. What a grand time to work justice in our churches rather than to be tempted by the General Board of Church and Society to beg Congress to act justly. I agree with my friend Stanley Hauerwas (tragically now an ex-United Methodist), who said that when the church is asked, "Say something political," we say "church." The church is God's odd answer to what's wrong with the world—not American, militarily sustained, capitalist democracy.

I have tried to reason with my state's congressional delegation, a couple of whom are United Methodists, and gotten nowhere. A much greater feat, even than calling our state's senators to account, would be for me to foster accountability among my colleagues on the COB. My attempts to joust with the state legislature suggested that my time would have been better spent preaching the gospel in our churches.

My great fear as a bishop was that I would wake up and be nothing more than a sanctified CEO. Personal devotions and Bible study, weekly visits to churches, constant opportunity for conversation with clergy and laity helped me stay focused on my chief vocation—to serve the Body of Christ rather than to efficiently manage a large volunteer organization. Eugene Peterson's word to pastors is perennially helpful to all of us clergy, including bishops who are so at risk for distraction from the main thing:

> There are a lot of other things to be done in this wrecked world and we are going to be doing at least some of them, but if we don't know the basic terms with which we are working, the foundational realities with which we are dealing—God, kingdom, gospel—we are going to end up living futile, fantasy lives. Your task is to keep telling the basic story, representing the presence of the Spirit, insisting on the priority of God, speaking the biblical words of command and promise and invitation.[4]

There is scant rationale—particularly in a church that needs so much administrative, executive change in so many areas—for retired bishops to continue to attend, to speak, and in various ways to attempt to steer the COB. No other human gathering insists that its executives work with their predecessors present beside them. The COB will continue to be unwieldy and ineffective as long as half the people in the room (retired bishops outnumber active) are no longer actively functioning as bishops.

The challenge our church faces with retired bishops is illustrated by retired bishops' "Statement of Counsel to the Church—2011,"[5] where the bishops condemn the *Discipline's* strictures against ordaining gay and lesbian clergy. It is notable that the statement (1) was mostly concerned with clergy, (2) was made up of signers who were all North American bishops, and (3) cost the signatories nothing.

Episcopal criticism of General Conference is a tricky proposition. A bishop dissing the *Discipline* is almost like a federal judge asserting the injustice of the Constitution that he or she is pledged justly to apply. When asked to respond to the "Statement of Counsel," Bishop Timothy W. Whitaker defended the denomination's position. "It's in agreement with Scripture and ecumenical Christian tradition . . . We have the Church—with a capital C—in many different cultural settings, and in those different cultural settings, there are different understandings of human sexuality . . . the Church must be mindful of its responsibility to its members in all its cultural settings and not just select ones." One suspects that the statement was designed to bypass the opposition of bishops in Africa with North American arguments for the centrality of sexuality.

If anyone asks why some active bishops seek to lessen the participation of retired bishops, the "Statement of Counsel" gives answer. Retired bishops have "voice but no vote" on the COB, but that doesn't diminish their dominance. (I kept an informal tally of who talked at the COB and how much. Retired bishops talk more.) One fellow bishop attributes the loquaciousness of the retirees to many having failed to achieve their goals while they were active bishops, so they continue to hammer away at their pet projects in the leisure of retirement. My theory is that people who have once had power—who are now disempowered by retirement—tend to be big talkers and advice givers. Like in this book.

I have never had enthusiasm for the *Discipline's* paragraphs that limit ordination to heterosexuals—finding little biblical support for making sexual orientation *the* defining characteristic of clergy. On my long list of desirable attributes for ordinands, sexuality is at the bottom. North American Methodism is already too tethered to the preoccupations of the upper classes, including their propensity to define humanity on the basis of sexual preference. However, as a bishop, I have few reservations fulfilling the laboriously

147

debated, every-four-years-debated-one-more-time will of General Conference.

What the retired bishops should have said is that they object to some of the statements in the *Discipline* on the ordained ministry because they arise out of a decidedly un-Methodist presumption that GC ought to enforce detailed, top-down restrictions upon the annual conference regarding whom the AC should ordain as a United Methodist pastor. Years ago it was said that the UMC had organized itself on the principle that "you can't trust anybody." If there's good worth doing, it's worth a law forcing everyone to do it. (Or retired bishops making a statement—without consulting their fellow bishops who are still working—forcing upon the church through decree that which they couldn't get through the church's legislative process.) The power to call and to vet our clergy is a job that has historically been wisely left to the AC. I fully trust the Board of Ordained Ministry of the North Alabama Conference prayerfully to decide who ought and ought not be pastors in the UMC. I even trust the California-Nevada Conference to do the same.

I'm excited by the proposals to reorganize the COB. Bishop John Schol, who has a great mind for organizational matters, has provided some creative leadership in the area of COB innovation. The proposed position of a president of the COB who is a set-aside bishop who gives general oversight and leadership to the council's work, who represents the council with other churches, and who chairs the (ill-considered) connectional table would help us execute our good ideas. Having our meetings more focused on the pressing work that we have before us, reducing the number of council committees, constantly holding up before ourselves the key indicators of conference vitality and freely sharing those numbers with one another in our vital congregations initiative are positive moves for the COB.

As the CTA Report says: *"We need a cadre of mutually committed, collaborative, turnaround leaders that (1) make a compelling case for daring, disciplined, and sustained actions and*

(2) demonstrate strong leadership to vividly change what we emphasize, and de-emphasize many treasured approaches and programs . . . that, though valued, do not lead to effectiveness in achieving difference and desired outcomes . . . This is not a time for leaders who are ambivalent, reluctant, or unwilling to walk forward with humility and courage."

BISHOP IN MOTION

Today's bishop spends lots of time in travel, which was exactly Asbury's intention. (Whether we are traveling to the right places for essential purposes is another matter.) From the days of Francis Asbury, United Methodist bishops are defined as part of a general, itinerant superintendency, protected through our 1808 Constitution. Bishops are leadership well suited to a church that wants always to be on the move rather than settled, dull, and parochial. Coke and Asbury explained why itinerancy is at the heart of Methodism: "Everything is kept moving as far as possible; and we will be bold to say, that, next to the grace of God, there is nothing like this for keeping the whole body alive from the centre to the circumference, and for the continual extension of that circumference on every hand."[6]

Bishops preserve the purest form of early Methodist itinerancy. When my preachers sometimes whined about their appointments, pleading an unwillingness to move to some undesirable locale, it was nice to be able to respond, "Believe it or not, Patsy and I are not living in Alabama because we wanted to. A 2:00 a.m. phone call sent us here without our input into the decision. At least I'm giving you better consultation than the jurisdictional episcopacy committee gave me. And, as you can see, our move here has worked out great."

We ought to return to the historic practice of bishops being elected by GC.[7] Jurisdictions were empowered in our 1939 union, a plan that was tainted by sinful regional and racially based compromises. After 1939, bishops, who were previously elected from and roamed all over the connection, were jurisdictionally confined, restricting our authority to "residential and presidential supervision" of the region where we are elected (¶47). Damage has been done to our general connection by the invention of jurisdictions. I smile when I'm referred to as "the resident bishop of the Birmingham Area," thinking of how seldom I trouble a bed in Birmingham.[8] (Explain to me why bishops are the only UM pastors who are, without exception, required to live in the conference housing?) Before 1939, Methodist bishops were expected to make appointments in their respective ACs no more than three years in a row—the fourth year of their quadrennium was to be spent elsewhere. In Methodism, "resident" and "located," are not our favorite words. One of the most frequently asked questions of me in my first four years was, "Are you settling in?" My answer: "God willing, no."

I was once gently reprimanded by a fellow bishop for having the temerity to "enter another bishop's area" without previous formal notification. I wanted to say, "Hey, your area is my area, and my area needs all the good teaching it can get, so come on in." Instead I said, "I didn't know that you longed to speak at a retreat for college students where they relegated me to an iron bunk and I ate food slopped on tin trays. Wish they had asked you rather than me."

While GC election of bishops would not guarantee that we would get any more adventurous or creative bishops, it would at least give the possibility of calling forth our best talent, overcoming the "native son or daughter" mentality. Factors like talent, experience, and gifts might again be more important in the election of bishops than popularity, safety, and local affection.

We have frequently received the good of sending a pastor to a church where a major factor in that pastor's successful, transformative leadership was that the pastor was not homegrown; the pastor had been sent from elsewhere. The people who are produced by a given culture are unlikely transformers of that culture. General church election and general church itineration could boost the possibility of having bishops who bring fresh eyes and ears to the task of conference renewal.

I favor term limits for bishops, or at least the same sort of retirement that other UM clergy enjoy.[9] There is no Wesleyan theological rationale for electing bishops for life. Bishop-for-life encourages us bishops to take on inappropriate, nonfunctional, sacerdotal and ontological definitions of the episcopacy that plague some of our sister churches. In The United Methodist Church, unlike Roman Catholic, Orthodox, and Anglican churches, bishops are not ordained to a third order. We are elders who work with elders to oversee elders. When our time functioning as bishops is done, why can't we go back to the conference where we once served and continue the best job in the world— being a UM elder?

The words I wrote more than a decade ago were more prescient that I could have known: "In a church that is overmanaged and underled, we desperately need our bishops to become leaders in the decentralization and creation of a new connection."[10]

One way that we could build in more accountability for bishops is to tie our remuneration to our financial leadership. I decided to pay each of my DSs differently, based on my assessment of their gifts, the demands of their districts, and their leadership contributions. This means that the salaries of those in the ministry of oversight were correlated a bit more closely to their productivity, the same way that salaries more or less function for our pastors.

Why pay all bishops the same salaries? The demands of our areas differ; our areas contribute financially to the mission of the church at different levels, and we come into the episcopacy with different talents. If I succeed in better stewardship of our conference resources, if I raise more money for the mission of the church, if my leadership leads to more disciples, I should be paid accordingly. I can gleefully advocate a system of episcopal pay based on results because the results of my leadership haven't been all that great. The highest level of apportioned giving that my nference achieved during my two quadrennia was 84 percent. ie reason Patsy and I gave a third of our income back to the irch was because we felt that I should have been paid no more n 84 percent of what a bishop from a 100 percent annual con-nce is paid and that I should not make much more salary than DSs.

We have some bishops who have fewer churches to oversee than some of my DSs. We also have some bishops who serve so few vital congregations that their conferences contribute far less to the episcopal fund than they receive. I have noted the increased energy and vitality, to say nothing of the financial boon, we received from reducing the number of our districts by 25 percent and reducing the actual number of DSs even further.[11] Why can't the general church do the same with bishops? I'm sure that the COB would function better if it were smaller and bishops would function better if our remuneration were more closely tied to what we actually do to make disciples of Jesus Christ for the transformation of the world.

As a bishop one must become accustomed to having everything you say and do analyzed and judged, often with complete misinformation or false attribution of motives. Pastors are subject to public scrutiny, but because pastors don't have the power to determine other people's futures, public analysis is not as intense. A bishop's statements are examined, inflated, conflated, and misconstrued. Though one may try, it is generally impossible to differentiate between voicing a "personal" opinion and being a spokesperson for the church.

At times my critics seemed willful in their misapprehension of my intentions. No wonder bishops become skilled in the cautionary art of saying nothing as if they were saying something. A bishop is a supremely official, public person; anybody who relishes privacy and solitude ought not apply. It is difficult to see how the work can be done without wholly committing one's time and energy, without attendant sacrifice of time with aging parents, or children and grandchildren, and good friends. "Self-care" for clergy is all the rage these days (playing into the hands of clerical narcissistic self-concern). If a heightened need for self-care is part of your ministry, forget the episcopacy. In short, the episcopacy is the sort of job that can only be attempted after a grueling campaign in which hundreds of Methodists have spent hours scrutinizing your life and every word you have written, in which they put your ministry to a vote, believing that all of this constitutes a summons by God to the episcopacy.

It is a truism that bishops find it difficult to have friends among those with whom we work. Bishops have virtually unlimited power to appoint clergy. Friendship (as Aristotle long ago noted) wilts among inequalities of power. Though the job of a bishop is to hold closely the church, few desire to hold closely a bishop. Woe be unto the bishop who "desires to be loved by the Church, rather than by Him," warns Gregory.[12]

With the exception of our power to appoint, the church wisely limits the power of bishops: we are elected by a representative gathering of both laity and clergy, we usually serve only eight years in an AC, we don't make polity, we can only interpret polity, we convene and preside at annual and jurisdictional conference and General Conference but never have a vote, we are watched over by the judicial council whereby anyone can challenge a bishop's rulings,[13] we are evaluated (sort of) and appointed (without the possibility of our refusal) by the jurisdictional episcopacy committee.

ELECTION OF BISHOPS

Gregory says, "the government of souls is the art of arts!"[14] While it is unseemly for a person to seek the office of bishop, says Gregory, worse sinners may be those who flee the episcopacy "for the sake of their own peace."[15] I know that even my worst day as a seminary professor and university chaplain was more placid than an average day in the office of bishop.

I like that Gregory, a monk at the time, while commending the constant cultivation of spiritual disciplines, rebukes those bishops who "in their eagerness for the pursuit of contemplation only, decline to be of service to the neighbor by preaching."[16] There is much to be said for the monkish arts of Sabbath-keeping and meditative introspection, unless one is a bishop. The peculiar service demanded of a bishop is excruciatingly official, public service. The truly humble, says Gregory, are those who forego their self-doubts and desire for peaceful solitude and instead "do not resist the divine decree" to be of service to Christ and his church.[17] Thus Paul, who was negative about supererogation, declared that anyone who seeks the office of bishop "desires a good work." (1 Tim. 3:1 NKJV)

My election as bishop—when one considers the vast paper trail that I dragged behind me—is testimonial that UMs (at least those in attendance at the southeastern jurisdictional conference of 2004) are a forgiving lot. The episcopacy, like many leadership jobs, requires complete, whole-hearted investment, seven days a week, with exhausting administrative demands and with meager time for self and family. Still, I know of no jurisdictional conference that has had difficulty finding dozens of candidates who eagerly stand for election.

The UMC process of electing bishops—that I earlier criticized as being degrading and conformist in nature—is amazingly functional. The grueling process of having to appear before dozens of groups, of having to make statements in many different settings, and having to participate in an ecclesiastical beauty contest, has its virtues. Why shouldn't the church take a good, close look at candidates for the episcopacy, forcing them to articulate who they are and what drives them toward this demanding job? I know of no effective bishop, particularly none effective in leading change, who is not blessed with a surfeit of political savvy. It is imperative that a bishop be adept at discovery of who has power and who is able to make things happen. The election process, though messy and grueling, is great training ground for the episcopacy.

Gregory notes the curious dynamic in which a bishop "is in trepidation of not being elected," but when elected begins to believe that the election was fully deserved.[18] Those who are elevated by the church to this office must engage in ruthless self-assessment, advises Gregory.[19] So I welcome the ruthless ecclesiastical assessment.

In high school, long before I was thinking about ministry, I read the wickedly funny *How to Become a Bishop Without Being Religious*, written by a talented satirist who was also a Methodist preacher. After advising the aspiring cleric on what sort of car to drive, what sort of spouse to marry—all to insure election as a bishop—the author closed the book with an admission of *"The unpredictable nature of electing assemblies,"* in which he counseled:

> The solemn assemblies which select the winners in the race for high ecclesiastical position are . . . somewhat unpredictable and occasionally capricious in their choices. In a world where fairness and common sense prevail, a man can reasonably expect that diligent planning and half a professional lifetime spent in unrelenting devotion to the cause of getting himself named to an office of supreme spiritual power will almost automatically insure his elevation . . . What happens to our democratic ideals if accidental qualities such as superior ability, outstanding intellectual equipment or bona fide spirituality tilt the balances when weighed against the diligent efforts of the man of unexceptional endowments but tireless zeal who sweats, struggles, sacrifices and strives to make himself over into a model of what the vast, pious churchgoing public insists it wants in its clergy? . . . these electing assemblies frequently ignore the just claims of a good, pious servant of the Lord like you who has overcome the handicaps of small beginnings, average talents and undistinguished intellectual and spiritual attainments by fashioning yourself into just the kind of clerical personality you have every reason to think that the church prefers, and be stampeded into selecting men who have made no such effort as you have made and who commend themselves only for their brilliance, natural leadership ability, scholarship, personal winsomeness, strength

of character, prophetic voice and/or other gifts . . . This is a dreary thought . . . But do not be dismayed. The odds are still very much in your favor . . . that your painful efforts to make of yourself a reasonable facsimile will issue in your being mistaken for the real thing.[20]

I have been immensely influenced by the ecclesiology of my friend Stanley Hauerwas. But being a bishop has made me wonder if I embraced too unreservedly Hauerwas's communitarian, positive ecclesiology. Stanley forms his theology on the basis of his ecclesiology. The church is the material basis of his ethics. His friend Rowan Williams idealistically contends, "Just as we can trust God because he has no agenda that is not for our own good, so we can trust the Church because it is . . . a community of active peacemaking . . . where no one exists in isolation . . . everyone is working steadily to release the gifts of others."[21] I'm surprised to hear this great theologian praise the church for its human effects rather than its divine nature, but unsurprised that Archbishop Williams has found leading the actual church with its messy mix of sin and sanctity, its occasional lapses into demonic rebellion against God, to be a disillusioning experience and that Stanley spends more time in academia than in church. Both the expectations of Jesus and the empirical reality of the church challenge any effort to heap unreserved praise upon the church.

Still, I have found the episcopacy to be a faith-engendering experience. My ecclesiology is now a healthier mix of respect for the church's emulsion of sin (including my sin) and God's gracious redemption. I wish every UM got to see the signs and wonders that I have witnessed. Jesus is busy reclaiming his world, even when we are not. When one witnesses a church receive a well-substantiated, fresh anointing of the Holy Spirit, a congregation rise from the dead and bear fruit again, ordinary people reclaim a sense of their vocation, a pastor discover that he or she is not only a good pastor but also a good leader, one witnesses God again acting like the God who created Israel, the God who remembered and delivered the slaves and made them a people, God's self-reiteration as Jesus, who called fisher folk, tax collectors, and prostitutes, God again made visible and believable as author of The UMC. To repeat one of Rowan Williams's best aphorisms, "If we aren't self-created," (and we believe that we are not) "we are answerable to a truth we don't produce."[22] I'm thankful that after Bishop Bill Morris announced, "There is an election," I got to answer to a truth greater than I could have come up with on my own.

CHAPTER TEN

BISHOPS AS GIFT OF GOD TO WESLEYAN CHRISTIANITY

Paul Leeland received a letter written in a shaky hand, on blue, flowered notepaper, saying, "Dear Bishop, I have two things on my heart to share: I pray that you will reconsider your decision to move our beloved pastor, and I hope that whoever is responsible will terminate you."

From the beginning, the notion of bishops within the Wesleyan movement has fought for credibility. As we noted, John Wesley himself said that he would rather be called a "knave" or a "fool" than a "bishop."

While most of this book has been a backward look at my episcopacy, the church is commanded by Christ to live forward into God's promised future. I am bold to believe that a chief way God will give our church a future is through bishops who are determined to serve God's future rather than maintain our institutional past. With a living God, we've always got more tomorrows than yesterdays. Toward the end of my career as self-styled gadfly and agitator, I find myself in the odd position of preaching that bishops are a primary reason why United Methodism's tomorrow could be even more interesting than its yesterday.

MY CHURCH LANGUISHES IN AN EXECUTORIAL CRISIS

We desperately need somebody to step up and, in service to our church, exercise agency. Fearful of the possibility of abuse of authority by those whom we elected bishops, we tried to run our church through committees, boards, and agencies headed by people who were elected by no one. Fears of authoritarian *episcope* led us to a crisis of authority. We got the organizational gridlock and sluggish bureaucracy we deserved. Few today cry, "Bishops are too powerful!" Rather it's, "Bishops have got to step up and 'bish!' " An overly legislated and regulated church tries to solve through rules and regulations the problems that only leadership can cure. No gutless committee ever made a really tough decision. The Methodist movement never intended itself to be led by anybody but bishops. When I asked my conference what they most needed from me, the reply was: "Somebody who can make a decision." The ill-conceived connectional table will never make our boards and agencies productive. Our bishops must oversee the general church, including a great reduction, realignment, and radical simplification of the mechanisms of our general church, including elimination of many of yesterday's great ideas for ministry.

Someone Must Take Responsibility for
Watching over the Church in Love

Bishops are "overseers," *epsicopoi*. The work that clergy do is too important to be unsupervised. Of course, bishops don't oversee alone, but a bishop alone has the responsibility to insure that supervision occurs. Half of my supervisory time was spent protecting clergy from laity and the other half protecting laity from clergy. I know a congregational church that spent over a year negotiating with and then expensively buying out their immoral pastor. As the pastor finally slithered out, the congregation split down the middle, half of them in sympathy with the adulterous pastor, the other half furious that it took so long to move against his egregious moral lapse. That would not have happened in a congregation of

The United Methodist Church, not because our clergy are never adulterous, but because we have bishops.

I've just told a pastor that he would move next month; he has been in a suburban congregation for nearly a year and has not received one new member. I've recently informed a pastor that we are unwilling for him to hang on another two years until his retirement; he can either take on a new, less demanding congregation or retire. I've also just informed a congregation that their pastor will be moving after two years; they have failed to step up and respond to their pastor's visionary leadership. "We have a surplus of pastors who have no vision for their ministry other than the care and comfort of self-centered congregations, so we will have a surfeit of pastors who will be a good fit for you. We need your present pastor in a church that wants to move forward." Those timely decisions would not have occurred in a non-UMC congregation for one reason: bishops.

Someone Must Lead New Means of Clergy and Congregational Accountability

A major function of the connection and of the annual conference specifically is to administer various mechanisms of holding pastors and churches accountable to the work of Christ. When there was a tsunami in Japan, it was the annual conference that got the attention of our congregations and provided them a specific, rapid way to respond. Only two or three of the new communities of faith that were started in our conference in my two quadrennia were begun at the initiative of an established congregation, and none were initiated without the guidance and training provided by the AC. Our most functional innovation—the North Alabama Conference Dashboard—is based on one of the oldest, most peculiar principles of Methodism: churches share with churches the fruits of their ministry. The Dashboard is a necessary component of a church that's both connected and overseen. Accountability begins with bishops quantifying the facts of ministry and making public the numbers.[1]

Someone Must Help Keep Church in Motion

Because we worship a God of the living and not the dead, because itinerancy is built deep into the practice of Methodist Christianity, bishops provide a major source of movement and disruption in a church that, like all churches, yearns for the comfort that comes from stability. No change occurs in a system without the infusion of energy and the introduction of disruption. Bishops are a primary way that happens in the UMC. If we hope to catch up with Jesus, we must step up the tempo. Bishops offer moribund, static congregations the gift of energy when we move clergy or when we refuse to move clergy, and a chance to face the truth about themselves and become more faithful. The church, making Jesus' mission primary, authorizes bishops to exercise the single most important power to change a system—the appointment of pastoral personnel. The quickest, surest way to produce change is by changing leadership.[2] Why does The UMC have more women in ministry than any other denomination? More clergy couples? Why, in spite of all the sociological odds against it, do we have a higher percentage of our established congregations now growing than do many other mainline denominations? Bishops! The Committee on General Conference is powerless to make any major change in the absurdly expensive, too-lengthy, nonproductive General Conference. Who must step up and save General Conference from itself? Bishops! Who will hold seminaries accountable for the clergy they produce? Bishops! Who can boldly recognize new, young talent and exit dysfunctional, ineffective clergy? You know who.

Someone Must Pray for and Signal
the Unity of the Church

This historic function of bishops is necessary for ecclesiastical change. Change often produces declension. The unity of church is not in homogeneity of race or economic status, nor is it a principle, rule, or form of organization, but rather is a person, Jesus Christ. The role of a UM bishop is inherently connectional and personal. Most UMs don't spend much time worrying about the state of UMs in New York or Nairobi, but bishops do. Our unity with God and with one another as Christians is personal, Jesus Christ. Our unity as a church is personal, a bunch of bishops whose concerns are connectional rather than congregational.

Someone Must Nurture and Teach Sound Doctrine
The bishops have made "Making Disciples" our denomination's mantra. Jesus said that we make disciples not only by baptizing but also by teaching. A bishop teaches not only in formal preaching and teaching opportunities but also in administration of the church. My second year as bishop I received a complaint from a layperson who was angry that his pastor had "prayed for Osama bin Laden" that past Sunday. When I asked the pastor how he could have done something so inflammatory to the sensibilities of the laity, he replied, "Bishop, I really believe that the crucified Jew who commanded, 'pray for those who persecute you' was the Son of God." Orthodox prayer begins in Christology. When our new governor stood in King's Dexter Avenue Baptist Church in Montgomery and declared, "I want to see each of you as my brother, but I can't unless you accept Jesus as your Savior," I attempted to counter with a bit of sound doctrine, noting that the only reason I regard the governor as my brother is because Jesus Christ has made me and the governor his brothers; my decision and his decisions didn't have a lot to do with it. I didn't mean to lecture our governor (he's a Baptist, so he could care less what a Methodist thinks). My intention was to remind United Methodists in Alabama how much more biblical is our Arminian theology than that of incipient, double predestination neo-Calvinism! Now who, but a bishop, would feel the need publically to correct the errors of a Baptist politician?

CHRIST AS A LEADERSHIP CRISIS

Everyone agrees that we are currently in a "crisis of leadership." Our numbers indicate that we have been under-led, or led in the wrong sorts of ways. Our indicators of institutional health say that we need to do some things differently.

But I remind you that the first and most enduring "crisis of leadership" is named "Jesus Christ." Jesus Christ assaulted our definitions of "God" and "Messiah," and disrupted and challenged our notions of leadership. From the first, he predicted that the people in charge would reject him. Those early predictions were quickly validated by the response of the authorities to Jesus.

From the first Jesus recruited odd leadership, surprising us by those he called to lead his movement. Those whom the world regarded as marginalized, ill-equipped, poorly informed, not particularly spiritual or moral, Jesus named as "disciples," confounding the worldly-wise, promising these losers glory in his coming kingdom. In the world, leaders must be omniscient and omnipotent, capable and courageous, competent and creative. Leaders in Jesus' name must simply be obedient to his "Follow me."

As bishop, I am frequently reminded by the Holy Spirit that Jesus was crucified through the leadership of people like me, persons in positions of spiritual authority over others. As bishop, I'm closer to Caiaphas than to Saint Paul. Therefore I have found it a salubrious practice to have close by me King's "Letter from Birmingham Jail," written to someone just like me.

The theological core of the Service of Ordination is the historic Veni Creator Spiritus, "Come, Holy Spirit," the epiclesis that the bishop prays for the ordinands. As I have repeatedly affirmed, ministry, in any of its forms, is too demanding to do alone. And yet, a prayer for the gift of the Holy Spirit is a dangerous request. The Holy Spirit descends not only with gifts but also with assignments. When the Holy Spirit enables intimacy with God, the Holy Spirit instigates the presence of the Trinity—all of the Trinity. That means that the Holy Spirit connects us not only with the creative Father but also with the suffering of the Son, not only with divine power but also with divinely humble service.

The only good reasons to be in any sort of ministry are theological. Sometimes we do theology reading books or listening to sermons and sometimes we do theology by getting our hands dirty, diving into the fray, and attending to the Body. The only hope we have for accomplishing anything in our church leadership is our faith that Jesus Christ really rose bodily from the dead and is on the move utilizing the same sorts of knuckleheads whom he first called and commissioned.

When I, midyear, appointed a pastor to a church that had been in unmitigated decline for two decades—right after removing a pastor whose ineffectiveness was exposed in his first three months at the church—and when I congratulated the pastor for effecting in a scant three months dramatic growth in attendance, membership, and giving, the pastor replied, "Thanks for having the courage to appoint me here. I've made a startling theological discovery in the past couple of months: we have a God who is even more able than I believed."

One reason many of our churches praise a rather trivial, allegedly concerned but essentially inactive God is that they haven't attempted anything so bold and brash that they risk utter, embarrassing failure *unless* the first Easter women were right and Jesus Christ really has risen from the dead. Hesitant, circumspect ecclesiological practice requires no better than a limp and trifling Christology.

Earlier I condemned the docetic temptation to disdain concern with administrative, managerial structures of the church—Jesus Christ is really, fully, completely human; disembodied faith is not faith in him.

I close this episcopal meditation by affirming that the mission of the church is utterly impossible without a Jesus who is really, fully, completely divine. His Body, though crucified, is where the fullness of God chooses to dwell. There is no God hiding behind the Incarnation, holding anything back from humanity. Jesus actually is God coming for us, God in motion, more God than we can handle, God refusing to be vague or insubstantial, God with a body, God so near as to demand human response. Any weakening of the divine in Christ results in indecision and uncertainty, a fatal, equivocal, indistinct vagueness that is the death of leadership in Jesus' name. Just as some wish that Jesus had not come as a Jew, had not refused self-defense and violence, had not turned his back on wealth and worldly power, had not said so many unkind things about religious leaders like me, many wish that Jesus had not made the poor old United Methodist Church his Body, his answer to what's wrong, an outbreak of the kingdom of God, his people saved from the world in order to be his means of saving the world.

The positive response to the errant Jesus Seminar by many Methodists shows that a tamed, West-Coast, solely human Jesus is in many ways appealing. But my experience of the episcopacy proves that no earthbound, purely human savior is Jesus. What God expects the church to do among suffering humanity can't be done by humanity alone. The kingdom of God is not devised by human efforts, even very skilled leadership. Any God who is less than the one who raised Jesus from the dead is no match for the deadly challenges facing The UMC. What God means to do among us is more, so much more, than even a well-functioning organization. So if God was not in Christ, reconciling the world, then being bishop is the dumbest of undertakings.

As my episcopacy wanes, I feel much like Moses on Mount Nebo. I've gotten a privileged, late-career glimpse of the promised land. I've seen Methodism's vital future. I've been able to participate, here and there, in what I believe will be the tomorrow of our church. (It only took God four hundred years to get around to rescuing the slaves from Egypt, so who am I to lament that I got so little accomplished in eight years as bishop?) If I live until 2050, which seems unlikely, I may enjoy the reality of a fully recovered and robust Wesleyanism. I believe that the patterns of episcopal oversight that I and some of my fellow bishops have begun shall bear fruit. If I'm wrong, you'll have to come to the basement of Duke Chapel, where I'll be entombed in order to mock me in my error; after this book you probably won't see me that often at the COB.

Those who say, "Willimon, you are not a good leader," have their point. I readily admit to many of my leadership liabilities (though I've discovered that some of what my critics label as leadership liabilities are, through the work of the Holy Spirit, God-induced assets). My only justification for being bishop is similar to that of any Methodist preacher—God put me here. I'm as surprised by God's call as my critics are. All Christian authority is open to question because it is authority that rests upon Christ's still-disputed sovereignty. According to Matthew 25, there will be surprises for all of us at the Great Assize. (In my worst nightmare it's me before the throne of Judgment, asking, "Lord, when did I see you?" and the King looking down at me, saying, "Surprise. Inasmuch as you smart-mouthed, castigated, and ridiculed the Institute on Religion and Democracy, you did it unto me. I love Mark Tooley as much as I love you.")

I think I'm obeying God's will in my episcopacy, but as with any disciple who struggles with self-deception, only God knows for sure.[3]

Still, in responding to Jesus' vocation, in attempting to conduct my life more in service to the needs of the church than my personal preferences, in trusting Jesus' faith in me more than my doubts about my abilities, Jesus' crisis of leadership becomes a grand adventure, leading not as the world leads but as Jesus commands.

For the good of the church (I hope) and for my great joy (most of the time), I was able to play a bit part in the great drama that is God's Incarnation in the world, God's loving determination not to work alone. It's a vocation I didn't deserve, but I shall always be grateful I got called. I got to be a bishop. Thanks, church. Isn't God's grace undeserved, strange, and amazing?

NOTES

Introduction

1. Quoted in Russell Richey with Dennis M. Campbell and William B. Lawrence, *Marks of Methodism: Theology in Ecclesial Practice* (Nashville: Abingdon Press, 2005), 11.

2. William H. Willimon, *Why I Am a United Methodist* (Nashville: Abingdon Press, 1990); *United Methodist Beliefs: A Brief Introduction* (Louisville: Westminster John Knox, 2007); and *This We Believe: The Core of Wesleyan Faith and Practice* (Nashville: Abingdon Press, 2010).

3. Russell E. Richey and Thomas Edward Frank, *Episcopacy in the Methodist Tradition* (Nashville: Abingdon Press, 2004), 25.

4. Our best contemporary Christian commentator on social change, James Davison Hunter, disputes romantic views of social change: "The deepest and most enduring forms of *cultural* change nearly always occur from the 'top down' . . . The work of world-making and world-changing are, by and large, the work of elites . . . who provide creative direction." James Davison Hunter, *To Change the World: The Irony, Tragedy, and Possibility of Christianity in the Late Modern World* (Oxford: Oxford University Press, 2010), 41.

5. George Weigel said much the same things about new Catholic bishops in "The End of the Bernardin Era: The Rise, Dominance, and Decline of a Culturally Accommodating Catholicism," *First Things* (February 2011).

6. Paul Borden said that bishops produce three key moments in the life of an annual conference: the end of a Bishop's term, the beginning of a Bishop's term, and the third year. Paul D. Borden, *Hit the Bullseye: How Denominations Can Aim the Congregation at the Mission Field* (Nashville: Abingdon Press, 2003), 48. This book's purpose is to enable my annual conference to get all the good it can out of my departure.

1. Body of Christ in Motion

1. *The United Methodist Book of Worship* (Nashville: The United Methodist Publishing House, 1992), 703.

2. Gil Rendle said that we bishops exemplify Jim Collins's "genius with a thousand helpers." Gil Rendle, *Journey in the Wilderness: New Life for the Mainline* (Nashville: Abingdon Press, 2010), 85.

3. Ron Heifetz, *Leadership Without Easy Answers* (Cambridge, MA: Harvard University Press, 1994), 231.

4. Aristotle quoted by Nannerl O. Keohane, *Thinking about Leadership* (Princeton, NJ: Princeton University Press, 2010), 60.

5. John P. Kotter, *Leading Change* (Cambridge, MA: Harvard Business School Press, 1996).
6. Robert L. Wilson and William H. Willimon, *Rekindling the Flame: Strategies for a Vital United Methodism* (Nashville: Abingdon Press, 1987).
7. In Earl G. Hunt Jr., *A Bishop Speaks His Mind* (Nashville: Abingdon Press, 1987), 78, the author warns that a bishop "must never play favorites" but must treat everyone equally and fairly. A leader has an obligation to identify and to empower those who can contribute value to the system.
8. The gift of connectionalism is explored in Russell E. Richey, *Methodist Connectionalism: Historical Perspectives* (Nashville: General Board of Higher Education and Ministry, The United Methodist Church, 2009).
9. Nelson Mandela, *Long Walk to Freedom: The Autobiography of Nelson Mandela* (New York: Little, Brown, 1994), 22.
10. The contemporary political history of my adopted state is documented in Allen Tullos, *Alabama Getaway: The Political Imaginary and the Heart of Dixie* (Athens: the University of Georgia Press, 2011).
11. Tullos, *Alabama Getaway*, 2.
12. Ibid., 3.
13. Methodist Susan Pace Hamill enlisted me in her fight against Alabama's tax code. See Susan Pace Hamill, *The Least of These: Fair Taxes and the Moral Duty of Christians* (Birmingham: Crane Hill, 2003).
14. I organized a Service of Repentance in the spring of 2012 in which we UMs repented for our role in the murder of Father Coyle.
15. See the list in Wayne Flynt, *Alabama in the Twentieth Century* (Tuscaloosa: University of Alabama Press, 2004), 470–72. I tried to make Flynt's history required reading for all clergy trying to understand the context of their ministry, particularly chap. 10, "What Would Jesus Do? Religion."
16. David T. Olson, *The American Church in Crisis* (Grand Rapids: Zondervan, 2008), 107.
17. Tullos, *Alabama Getaway*, 248.

2. Summoned to Be Bishop

1. Nannerl O. Keohane, *Thinking about Leadership* (Princeton, N.J.: Princeton University Press, 2010), 19.
2. Rupert Shortt, *Rowan's Rule: The Biography of the Archbishop of Canterbury* (Grand Rapids: William B. Eerdmans, 2009), 240.
3. Saint Gregory, *Pastoral Care*, circa 590.
4. Ibid., 41.
5. William H. Willimon, *Calling and Character: Virtues of the Ordained Life* (Nashville: Abingdon Press, 2000).
6. Barbara J. Blodgett, *Lives Entrusted: An Ethic of Trust for Ministry* (Minneapolis: Fortress, 2008), chap. 3.
7. "We then rode to Baltimore, where we met a few preachers: it was agreed to form ourselves into an Episcopal Church, and to have superintendents, elders, and deacons. When the conference was seated, Dr. Coke and myself were unanimously elected to the superintendency of the Church, and my ordination followed . . ." was Asbury's curt account of the birth of Wesleyan bishops. Russell

Richey, Kenneth E. Rowe, and Jean Miller Schmidt, *The Methodist Experience*, 49.

8. I'm indebted for the following highlights of the birth of Wesleyan bishops to John Wigger, *American Saint: Francis Asbury and The Methodists* (New York: Oxford University Press, 2009), 161-62, 189.

9. Thomas Coke, "The substance of a sermon preached at Baltimore, Maryland before the General Conference of The Methodist Church, December 27, 1784 at the ordination of the Rev. Francis Asbury, to the office of a superintendent." (New York; Published at the desire of the Conference by T. Mason and G. Lane, 1784.)

10. Wigger, *American Saint: Francis Asbury and the Methodists*, 229–30.

11. Edward Leroy Long Jr., *Patterns of Polity* (Cleveland: Pilgrim, 2001), 29.

12. Lovett Weems makes "address the cost of General Conference" one of his key ideas for improving the future of our church. He also advocated linking general church spending to accountability for outcomes, not to the production of activities, stressing the urgent need for episcopal oversight of the general church. (See Lovett H. Weems, *Focus: The Real Challenges That Face The United Methodist Church* [Nashville: Abingdon Press, 2012], chap. 3.) I was gratified to see so much agreement with Weems on many of my prescriptions.

13. See Francis Sullivan, *From Apostles to Bishops: The Development of the Episcopacy in the Early Church* (Mahwah, NJ: Paulist, 2001).

14. Larry M. Goodpaster, *There's Power in the Connection: Building a Network of Vital Congregations* (Nashville: Abingdon Press, 2008).

15. The COB's Call to Action says that "the Church rewards administrative/maintenance behaviors—risk taking is neither encouraged nor rewarded." http://umc.org/calltoaction.

16. Tertullian, crabby critic of ecclesial hierarchy, admitted that no less an authority than the Holy Spirit whispered into Ignatius's ear: "Do nothing without the Bishop." (E. R. Dodds, *Pagan and Christian in an Age of Anxiety* [Cambridge, UK: Cambridge University Press, 1965], 66.)

3. Bishops Sending Pastors

1. Shakespeare, *Twelfth Night*, act 2, sc. 5.

2. In Larry Goodpaster, *There's Power in the Connection* (Nashville: Abingdon Press), 71, Larry stated: "The *conference* does not make disciples, but the conference-level leadership (starting with the bishop) can create an atmosphere of expectation that every local church will *thrive* and *make disciples* and *be alive.*"

3. North Alabama not only has a great tradition of mission engagement but is also home to the jurisdictional office of United Methodist Volunteers in Mission as well as the world center of Servants in Faith and Technology, a home-grown Christian development organization that provides training and equipment of missionaries around the world.

4. See Christian A. Schwarz, *Natural Church Development* 7th ed. (Carol Stream, IL: ChurchSmart Resources, 2006). www.NCD-international.org.

5. I had each DS read Marcus Buckingham and Curt Coffman, *First, Break All the Rules* (Simon and Schuster, 1999). A DS could easily take *First, Break*

All the Rules and everywhere "manager" is used substitute "DS" and have one of the finest guidebooks to be a top-functioning DS.

6. Bishop Hunt lists "a wholesome and satisfying sex life" as very important for the successful pastor. Yikes. Earl G. Hunt Jr. *A Bishop Speaks His Mind: A Candid View of United Methodism* (Nashville: Abingdon, 1987), 75.

7. The Strengths Profile is a report that comes after taking a questionnaire that indicates a person's five strengths in leadership. The Strengths Profile is a nationally tested instrument that is discussed in the widely acclaimed book by Marcus Buckingham and Don Clifton, *Now, Discover Your Strengths* (Boston: Free Press, 2001). Their thesis is that organizations worry about people's weaknesses without focusing upon their strengths. The good employer plays to people's strengths, rather than attempting to put them in unrealistic positions where they must overcome their weaknesses. The Cabinet learned so much from the Strengths Profile that we asked every pastor to use the profile. (By the way, my strengths were maximizer, strategizer, and ideation, to the surprise of no one who knew me.)

8. I cling to William James's definition of intelligence as the bold willingness to make a decision even before all the facts are known. *Thinking about Leadership* has helped me in these thoughts on judgment and leadership. Nannerl O. Keohane, *Thinking about Leadership* (Princeton: Princeton University Press, 2010), 90–96.

9. We got the idea for this program from the book by Michael Watkins, *The First Ninety Days: Critical Success Strategies for New Leaders at All Levels* (Boston: Harvard Business School Press, 2003).

10. The massive Duke Divinity School Clergy Health Initiative says that many clergy complain about being under stress. (http://divinity. duke.edu/initiatives-centers/clergy-health-initiative) I know firsthand that ordained leadership in the name of Jesus is stressful work. However, I also have found that clergy who lack the talent and the skill to do the work that growing the church demands are often overstressed. More important than overstressing clergy stress is to identify and fully utilize clergy who thrive in service to an expansive kingdom.

11. Kate Willson, "40 Years After Peter Principle, Promotions Still Aren't a Science," *Business Pundit.* Accessed November 21, 2011. http://www.businesspundit.com/40-years-after-peter-principle-promotion-still-arent-a-sciences.

12. John Wigger, *American Saint: Francis Asbury and the Methodists* (Oxford: Oxford University Press, 2010).

4. Bishops Cultivating Fruitfulness

1. I like the distinction between "success" and "fruitfulness" made by Lovett H. Weems Jr. and Tom Berlin in *Bearing Fruit: Ministry with Real Results* (Nashville: Abingdon, 2011).

2. See Sprague, Bishop C. Joseph. *Affirmations of a Dissenter* (Abingdon, 2002) or http://ucmpage.org/news/sprague_heresy11.html.

3. Bishop Tuell says that we are organized "to have as many people as possible participate in decision-making." Jack M. Tuell, *Organization of The UMC* (Nashville: Abingdon Press, 2010), 8.

4. Jim Collins makes the helpful distinction between representation and execution types of organization. Jim Collins, *Good to Great and the Social Sectors* (New York: HarperCollins, 2005), 11.

5. See John Wesley, "Nature, Design, and Rules of the United Societies" in *The Book of Discipline of the United Methodist Church* (Nashville: The United Methodist Publishing House). Emphasis mine.

6. Patrick Lencioni, *Three Signs of a Miserable Job: A Fable for Managers (and Their Employees)* (San Francisco: Jossey-Bass, 2007). Our Cabinet utilized an early book by Patrick Lencioni, *The Five Dysfunctions of a Team* (San Francisco: Jossey-Bass, 2002) to analyze health as a team. We scored low on "trust," made some changes, and our score improved.

7. Lencioni, *Three Signs*, 128.

8. Ibid., 131.

9. By the way, in every one of these congregations, middle-aged pastors had led these congregations to decline. Every one of these younger pastors led growth; some of them led dramatic growth in the first year. Pastors who have graduated from seminary in the past fifteen years seem to have greater skills in leading growth than pastors who were trained in the 1970s and 1980s.

10. Why must every conference publish a conference journal? The numbers in the journal are expensive to collect, irrelevant, and dated. Ironically, the directive to concoct an expensive, laborious, printed collection of so much data ensures that we will never notice the most important data.

11. Gil Rendle lists "the assumption that ministry can't be measured" as a major factor in ecclesiastical dysfunction. Gil Rendle, *Journey in the Wilderness* (Nashville: Abingdon Press, 2010), 125–27. When the *United Methodist Reporter* did a story on our Dashboard, a pastor from Peoria said that he preached a sermon on the need to reach out to the poor and asked, "How can you measure that?" Duh.

12. See my plea for "An Affirmative Action Program for United Methodists," http://www.northalabamaumc.org/blogs/detail/209. The General Commission on Religion and Race, as Black Methodists for Church Renewal, appear to limit themselves to clerical concerns and show no interest in increasing the number of African American UMs. During the years that we have had a GCRR, while a couple of groups have had modest growth in The UMC (Koreans and Spanish-speaking), the proportion of African Americans in The UMC has continued to drop. The bishops' "Making disciples for the transformation of the world" means nothing.

13. "Address to the Clergy" (1756), in *Works* (Jackson) 10:480–500.

14. Data is only a tool for assessment. Mere numbers can't tell us what to do or how to do it. Friedman condemned modernity's "almost panicky obsession with data and technique" in which "leaders tend to rely more on expertise than on their own capacity to be decisive." Edwin H. Friedman, *A Failure of Nerve: Leadership in the Age of the Quick Fix* (The Edwin Friedman Estate/Trust, 6 Wynkoop Court, Bethesda, MD 20817, 1999), 11. The collection and dissemination of data through mechanisms such as our Dashboard make leadership of the church as difficult and decisive as Jesus intends.

15. Our stress on quantification of ministry is based on traditional Wesleyan habits and confirms the management dictum that "successful adaptive changes

build on the past rather than jettison it." Ronald A. Heifetz, Alexander Grashow, and Marty Linsky, *The Practice of Adapative Leadership* (Boston: Harvard Business School Publishing, 2009), 15.

16. According to Peter F. Drucker, "Nonprofit institutions tend not to give priority to performance and results. Yet performance and results are far more important—and far more difficult to measure and control—in the nonprofit institution than in a business." Peter F. Drucker, *Managing the Nonprofit Organization: Principles and Practices* (New York: Harper Collins, 1990), 61. The night I read Drucker's chapter, "What is the Bottom Line When There is No Bottom Line?" was the genesis of my interest in metrics for ministry.

17. Bishop Tuell says that the Committee on the Episcopacy "provides an important check against possible abuses of power by bishops." Jack M. Tuell, *The Organization of the United Methodist Church: 2005–2008 Edition* (Nashville: Abingdon Press, 2005), 39. We have a problem of power abuse by bishops? *Effective* bishops ought to be the main concern.

18. If you doubt that the Council of Bishops has dramatically changed, read Roy H. Short, *History of the Council of Bishops of the United Methodist Church* (Nashville: Abingdon Press, 1980), a description of bishops in another world. It is inconceivable that the Call to Action Report could have been produced for the COB before 2004.

19. Shortly after the CTA appeared, critics launched a predictable attack. Patricia Farris charged that the CTA's "ecclesiology is thin and operational" in researchers' measurement of "membership" and "worship attendance," encouraging "idolatry and competition." Farris dismisses these "outmoded categories," failing to mention *anything* worth counting. Farris served as a DS and said she now wishes she had "spent more time in pastoral care with my pastors and less in the latest revitalization workshops" (see "Church Vitality Is Not Just a Matter of Numbers," *The United Methodist Church Portal* [Nov. 29, 2010]. Accessed January 12, 2012. http://www.umc.org/site/apps/nlnet/content3.aspx?c=lwL4Kn N1LtH&b=2789393&ct=8933913).

20. Hendrik R. Pieterse criticized the CTA for its lack of theological substance, a criticism with which I agree. But when he offered his theology, it was, "hospitality to the marginalized." Pieterse failed to notice that the CTA arose from the bishops' concern for the nearly three million women and men, mostly youth and children, and lots of straights, gays, and the poor who have not been shown hospitality by our church in the past twenty years. "In Praise of Bureaucracy: Mission, Structure, and Renewal in The United Methodist Church," Occasional Papers, No. 103, December 2010, The General Board of Higher Education and Ministry, The United Methodist Church.

5. Bishops Leading Change

1. Eberhard Busch, *Barth* (Nashville: Abingdon Press, 2008), 20.

2. Jason Vickers (in his excellent *Minding the Good Ground: A Theology for Church Renewal* (Waco, TX: Baylor University Press, 2011) called my attention to E. R. Dodds's comment (in *Pagan and Christian in an Age of Anxiety* [Cambridge, UK: Cambridge University Press, 1965], 2) that bishops were foes of the Holy Spirit in the Montanist controversy so that, due to bishops, the Holy

Spirit "ceased in practice to play any audible part in the counsels of the Church." Is that why anti-bishop Wesley said that he suspected that "arch-heretic, Montanus, was one of the holiest men of the second century"? (Vickers, *Minding the Good Ground*, 1). Did Wesley oppose bishops because of his vigorous pneumatology?

3. Robert Schnase, foreword to *Journey in the Wilderness: New Life for Mainline Churches*, by Gil Rendle (Nashville: Abingdon Press, 2010), ix.

4. Some of my earliest reactions to the episcopacy are found in: William Willimon, "First-Year Bishop: Dispatch from Birmingham," *Christian Century* 122, no. 19 (September 20, 2005): 28–31.

5. Preamble, 21.

6. "The purpose of the annual conference is to make disciples of Jesus Christ for the transformation of the world by equipping its local churches for ministry and by providing for ministry beyond the local church, all to the glory of God." See ¶601, *The Book of Discipline of The United Methodist Church* (Nashville: United Methodist Publishing House).

7. I would change one word: "every" is an unrealistic expectation. Many congregations have lost the capacity (judging from their record of fruitfulness) to make more disciples for Jesus Christ.

8. Once I filled my Cabinet with activists and initiators, Gil Rendle warned me never to allow a DS to take on some new responsibility without first identifying what task the DS would stop doing.

9. Gil Rendle rightly contends, "a church responds best when it recognizes what is essential, what is primary." *Journey in the Wilderness*, 5. Vision helped us keep the main thing the main thing.

10. The CTA is inconceivable without the change that has occurred in annual conferences, principally in the South Central and Southeastern Jurisdictions.

11. Clayton M. Christensen, *Seeing What's Next: Using the Theories of Innovation to Predict Change* (Boston: Harvard Business School Publishing, 2004).

12. King's Birmingham jail letter: http://www.africa.upenn.edu/Articles _Gen/Letter_Birmingham.html.

13. See the account of the lives of the recipients of King's letter in Jonathan Bass, *Blessed Are the Peacemakers: Martin Luther King Jr., Eight White Religious Leaders, and the "Letter from Birmingham Jail"* (Baton Rouge: Louisiana State University Press, 2001).

14. In nearly three hundred sermons, I received no more than a dozen letters of thanks from host pastors. Of course, none of these servants of the servants of God are thanked for their ministry either. Service is expected of the ordained (see Luke 17:9).

15. Commitment to conversion is one of the greatest theological gifts we Wesleyans have to offer the Body of Christ, a challenge to all theologies of accommodation and contentment. The God who meets Wesleyans in Jesus Christ is enemy of the status quo. Or as Barth put it, *Gott nimmer ruhet* (God never rests). See my concluding essay in Kenneth J. Collins and John H. Tyson, *Conversion in the Wesleyan Tradition* (Nashville: Abingdon Press, 2001).

16. Theological Declaration of Barmen, in *Book of Confessions: Study Edition* (Louisville, KY: Geneva Press, 1996), 311.

17. Bishop Suda Devedar's conference elected a diverse General Conference delegation composed entirely of first-time GC delegates. Many bishops told me that they would not tolerate a delegation composed of people who were unable to lead in connectional giving. As I said, I'm not the most successful of bishops!

18. I had the good fortune to grow in ministry in a conference where, as a young clergyperson, my gifts were affirmed and I was given grand opportunities to lead and to grow in my ministry. A sign of a healthy organization is the willingness of the dominant generation graciously to step aside and call to the fore the new talent needed to produce the future. I am ashamed of the way that my generation is threatened by young UMs.

19. http://www.wmbridges.com/training/training-lead_org_trans.html.

20. Gil Rendle noted how long-established congregations and church systems tend to stick with a strategy long after it has been shown, by lack of results, unworkable. They exchange love of strategy for loyalty to purpose. Rendle, *Journey in the Wilderness*, 23.

21. Edwin H. Friedman, *A Failure of Nerve: Leadership in the Age of the Quick Fix* (The Edwin Friedman Estate/Trust, 6 Wynkoop Court, Bethesda, MD 20817, 1999), 113.

22. Ibid., 176.

23. Russ Richey claimed that after our 1939 union, Southern bishops made the COB "a great fraternity," dedicating "their gatherings to social and peer-support functions. They treated one another with codes of 'southern' deference and courtesy. They became an extended family." Russell Richey, Kenneth E. Rowe, Jean Miller Schmidt, *The Methodist Experience,* 517. Blame us Southerners.

24. Gil Rendle, *Journey in the Wilderness*, xii, identified focus on relationships as the major impediment to mission in a congregation. Because most bishops' leadership experience only is as parish pastors, we tend to stress relationships because, as Gil noted, "congregations . . . give preference and priority to relationships" (54). There is no way the COB can be a "church" or a "family," two metaphors that are routinely (mis)applied to the COB.

25. The doggedly persistent minds of bishops Scott Jones, Janice Huie, Greg Palmer, John Schol, John Hopkins, Sally Dyck, Hope Morgan Ward, Mike Lowry, Robert Schnase, Jim Dorff, and Larry Goodpaster leap to mind.

26. Francis Asbury, first bishop of our church, made the constant movement of preachers a Methodist theological principle. A pastor with long tenure robbed the laity of their baptismally mandated ministry and was an offense against the active, energetic Holy Spirit. John Wigger, *American Saint: Francis Asbury and the Methodists* (New York: Oxford University Press, 2009).

27. Ronald Heifetz, Alexander Grashow, and Marty Linsky, *Leadership*, 26. Heifetz spoke of the "elegance and tenacity" of the status quo.

28. Chip Heath and Dan Heath, *Switch: How to Change Things When Change is Hard* (New York: Broadway Books, 2010), 123.

6. Bishops Body Building

1. It wasn't the annual conference that abandoned people in our inner cities; we UMC clergy became so expensive to maintain, so unsuited to ministry to the mar-

ginalized, that by training and inclination we limited the scope of God's grace. While we failed to retake McCoy as a congregation, we did attract a young man who was called to live in west Birmingham, raise much of his salary from donors, and begin The Church Without Walls. A second-career clergywoman began Genesis, a church in a former grocery store that specializes in being a church of the marginalized, particularly those with addictions. Another clergywoman founded One Eighty, a church for people who need to make a total turn in their lives. Then there's Innerchange UMC, meeting in a former warehouse, giving hard-working blue-collar folk the dynamic church they deserve. Wesleyanism lives!

2. Conversation with Russell Richey, January 7, 2011.

3. The metaphor "foundation repair and reinforcement" is used to describe the important work we have before us in Kenneth L. Carder and Laceye C. Warner, *Grace to Lead: Practicing Leadership in the Wesleyan Tradition* (Nashville: Abingdon Press, 2011).

4. See Jim Collins, *How the Mighty Fall: Why Some Companies Never Give In* (New York: HarperCollins, 2009), in which the author demonstrates how decline follows inattentiveness to core identity.

5. Lovett Weems said he believes that most renewed congregations resemble the next generation of a family more than an entirely new species. *Take the Next Step: Leading Lasting Change in the Church* (Nashville: Abingdon Press, 2003), 69.

6. All of *us* retired bishops must trust those who are currently charged with the active leadership of the church. The COB struggles to have urgent discussion and bold strategy. Even if this is an unintended result, input from retired bishops impedes the forward, adaptive movement of the COB, attempting to recall us to a more comfortable past. I hope this book on my way out will encourage those who are still in the saddle.

7. Ken Blanchard et al., *Who Killed Change?* (New York: William Morrow, 2009), 132-34.

8. Thomas G. Bandy, *Mission Mover: Beyond Education for Church Leadership* (Nashville: Abingdon Press, 2004).

9. Stanley M. Hauerwas and William H. Willimon, *Resident Aliens: Life in the Christian Colony* (Abingdon Press: Nashville, 1989).

10. See Thomas G. Bandy, *Roadrunner: The Body in Motion* (Nashville: Abingdon Press, 2002). You can learn more at Easum, Bandy and Associates at www.easumbandy.com.

11. See Thomas G. Bandy, *Coaching Change: Breaking Down Resistance, Building Up Hope* (Nashville: Abingdon Press, 2000).

12. Lyle Schaller, *The Ice Cube is Melting* (Abingdon Press, 2005). 76.

13. Ibid., 77.

14. Earl G. Hunt Jr., *A Bishop Speaks His Mind* (Nashville: Abingdon Press, 1987), 87.

15. In the U.S. the average congregation has seventy-five people in worship whereas the average U.S. Christian worships in a church that averages four hundred in attendance. Mark Chaves, *How Do We Worship?* (Herndon, VA: Alban Institute, 1999), 9-11.

16. Craig Kenneth Miller, *Seven Myths of the United Methodist Church* (Nashville: Discipleship Resources, 2008), 19.

17. See Charles Marsh's Berlin lecture on March 12, 2010, at the American Academy in Berlin. See http://www.americanacademy.de/home/audiovideo-archive/video/313//charles_marsh/.

18. My former teacher, Colin Williams, made a comment that has now become common folk wisdom: "Methodism is long on organization and short on theology." Colin W. Williams, *John Wesley's Theology Today* (Nashville: Abingdon Press, 1960), 5.

19. Carder and Warner,

20. According to Gil Rendle, "Corporations have a commitment to orderliness and structure, to predictable decision making, and to the centralization of authority." Gil Rendle, *Journey in the Wilderness: New Life for Mainline Churches* (Nashville: Abingdon Press, 2010), 69.

21. Jones pointed me to a very helpful book: Scott Belsky, *Making Ideas Happen: Overcoming the Obstacles Between Vision and Reality* (New York: Viking, 2011). John Wesley taught that organizational mechanisms like the charge conference were "means of grace," an amazing claim for structure.

22. "In the *not-for-profit sector*, organizations are typically mission driven. They tend to value consensus decision making, with everyone having a voice in tough decision making." That sounds like good, representational democracy. Then Heifetz added, "That also gives everyone a veto." Ronald Heifetz, Alexander Grashow, and Marty Linsky, *The Practice of Adapative Leadership* (Boston: Harvard Business School Publishing, 2009), 53.

23. Lyle Schaller, *The Ice Cube Is Melting* (Abingdon Press, 2005). 66. The CTA says that "Lack of accountability was also cited as a root cause of distrust—when people are not accountable for their actions and behaviors, they cannot be trusted."

24. James E. Dittes, "Administration vs. Ministry," in *Re-Calling Ministry*, ed. Donald Capps (St. Louis: Chalice Press, 1999), 107-22.

7. Bishops Preaching

1. Only one bishop biography gives major attention to preaching: Edsel A. Ammons, Ernest S. Lyght, and Jonathan D. Keaton, *The Confessions of Three Ebony Bishops* (Nashville: Abingdon Press, 2008), chaps. 3–4. These African American bishops also emphasize prayer. Both emphases (prayer and preaching) suggest to me that these bishops were determined not to be restricted by a corporate America style of leadership. Woodie W. White's *Confessions of a Prairie Pilgrim* (Nashville: Abingdon Press, 1988) shows a preaching bishop whose commitment to racial justice energized his leadership.

2. "The task of leaders is to guide the people to have conversations about the right things." Gil Rendle, *Journey in the Wilderness: New Life for Mainline Churches* (Nashville: Abingdon Press, 2010), 41.

3. "Finding themselves worshiped by others, they become worshipers of themselves," was how John Stuart Mill characterized a ruler's susceptibility to vanity. Quoted in Nannerl O. Keohane, *Thinking about Leadership* (Princeton, NJ: Princeton University Press, 2010), 209.

4. St. Gregory the Great, *Pastoral Care*, circa 590, 61.

5. "Listening from the heart is particularly difficult when you are in a position of authority . . . by the time you rise through the organizational or political system to a higher-level role you have probably been trained to talk more than to listen." Ronald A. Heifetz, Alexander Grashow, and Marty Linsky, *The Practice of Adaptive Leadership* (Boston: Harvard Business School Publishing, 2009), 268.

6. Max Weber said the source of leadership vanity was "the need personally to stand in the foreground as clearly as possible." Quoted in Keohane, *Thinking about Leadership*, 204–5.

7. Keohane, *Thinking about Leadership*, 206.

8. A selection of my weekly messages has been published as *The Will to Lead*, ed. Bryan Langlands (Nashville: Abingdon, 2011).

9. http://willimon.blogspot.com/ ("Peculiar Prophet"). A student at Asbury Theological Seminary maintains a twitter account with some of my quotes at twitter.com/NotWillWillimon.

10. St. Gregory the Great, *Pastoral Care*.

11. Gil Rendle said that clarity about identity is a key component in a vital congregation, whether that identity is conservative, liberal, or Pentecostal. See *Journey into the Wilderness*, 36.

12. "Letter from the Steering Team," as introduction to the CTA Report.

13. "When you set small, visible goals, and people achieve them, they start to get into their heads that they can succeed." Chip Heath and Dan Heath, *Switch: How to Change Things When Change is Hard* (New York: Broadway Books, 2010), 144.

14. Few contemporary UM pastors read widely (Wesley would scorn them). I couldn't tell that my authorial endeavors much interested my conference. In case you are interested, here are the books I published while bishop:

Peculiar Prophet: Will Willimon and the Craft of Preaching, ed. Will Malambri and Michael Turner (Nashville: Abingdon Press, 2004).

Sermons from Duke Chapel, ed. HWill Willimon (Durham, NC: Duke University Press Books, 2005).

Theology and Proclamation (Nashville: Abingdon Press, 2005).

Sinning Like a Christian: A New Look at the Seven Deadly Sins (Nashville: Abingdon Press, 2005).

Conversations with Barth on Preaching (Nashville: Abingdon Press, 2006).

Thank God It's Friday: The Seven Last Words of Jesus from the Cross (Nashville: Abingdon Press, 2007).

United Methodist Beliefs: A Brief Introduction (Louisville: Westminster John Knox, 2007).

Who Will Be Saved? (Nashville: Abingdon Press, 2008).

The Wesley Study Bible, ed. Will Willimon and Joel Green (Nashville: Abingdon, 2009).

Undone by Easter: Keeping Preaching Fresh (Nashville: Abingdon Press, 2009).

The Early Sermons of Karl Barth (Louisville: Westminster John Knox, 2009).

This We Believe: The Core of Wesleyan Faith and Practice (Nashville: Abingdon Press, 2010).

Preaching Master Class (Eugene, OR: Cascade Books, 2010). *The Collected Sermons of William H. Willimon* (Louisville: Westminster John Knox, 2010). *Why Jesus?* (Nashville: Abingdon Press, 2010. *The Will to Lead*, ed.. Bryan Langlands (Nashville: Abingdon, 2011). While I was an active bishop, other bishops engaged in serious writing: Larry Goodpaster, *There's Power in the Connection: Building a Network of Dynamic Congregations* (Nashville: Abingdon Press, 2008); Scott Jones, *United Methodist Doctrine: The Extreme Center* (Nashville: Abingdon Press, 2002); *Staying at the Table: The Gift of Unity for United Methodists* (Nashville: Abingdon Press, 2006); Walter Klaiber, *Justified Before God: A Contemporary Theology* (Nashville: Abingdon Press, 2006); and Robert Schnase published a dozen books on his "fruitful practices," beginning with *Five Practices of Fruitful Congregations* (Nashville: Abingdon Press, 2007).

15. Rendle, *Journey in the Wilderness*, 53.

16. Heifetz, Grashow, and Linsky, *The Practice of Adapative Leadership*, 15.

17. In the book by Ron Susskind, *Confidence Men: Wall Street, Washington and the Education of a President* (New York: HarperCollins, 2011), the author shows how Obama took a long time to figure out that a president's main job is to make tough decisions. Obama, according to Susskind, for too long lived by the vain hope that if he surrounded himself with intelligent, hard-working people, they would come to brilliant compromises that wouldn't require his painful decision.

18. Mickey Connolly and Richard Rianosher, *The Communication Catalyst* (Chicago: Dearborn Trade, 2002).

19. Chip Heath and Dan Heath, *Made to Stick: Why Some Ideas Survive and Others Die* (New York: Random House, 2007), 33–34.

20. Ken Blanchard and John Britt, *Who Killed Change?* (New York: William Morrow, 2009), 132.

21. Rupert Shortt, *Rowan's Rule: The Biography of the Archbishop of Canterbury* (Grand Rapids: Eerdman's, 2009).

22. The Heaths tell business leaders that storytelling is important transformative work. Every preacher knows that listeners remember only the illustrations and the stories an hour after the sermon ends. Isolated, abstract, non-narrated ideas don't stick. A leader gets people's attention (surprise), helps them understand and remember the idea (concrete), gives them the means to believe in the idea (credible), to care about the idea (emotional), and to be able to act (story). Heath and Heath, *Made to Stick*, 246–47.

8. Bishops Teaching

1. Not that Alabama Methodists showed great enthusiasm for my teaching. Notwithstanding my weekly e-mail messages and my series throughout the conference, I taught more outside my conference than within. Perhaps a bishop's administrative, appointive power detracts from a bishop's pedagogical role?

2. Gil Rendle, *Journey in the Wilderness: New Life for the Mainline* (Nashville: Abingdon Press, 2010), chaps. 2–3.

3. Ibid., 35.

4. Ronald A. Heifetz, *Leadership Without Easy Answers* (Cambridge, MA: Harvard University Press, 1994), 5.

5. Ibid., 112–13.

6. "Adaptive leadership is the practice of mobilizing people to tackle tough challenges and thrive." Ibid., 14.

7. Ronald Heifetz, Alexander Grashow, and Marty Linsky, *The Practice of Adapative Leadership* (Boston: Harvard Business School Publishing, 2009), 44–45.

8. Heifetz, *Leadership Without Easy Answers,* 254.

9. The thought is from Chip Heath and Dan Heath, *Switch: How to Change Things When Change is Hard* (New York: Broadway Books, 2010), 11.

10. Heifetz, Grashow, and Linsky, *The Practice of Adapative Leadership.*

11. Nannerl O. Keohane, *Thinking about Leadership* (Princeton, NJ: Princeton University Press, 2010), 54.

12. Heifetz, *Leadership Without Easy Answers,* 14–15.

13. George G. Hunter III, *Leading and Managing a Growing Church* (Nashville: Abingdon Press, 2000), 25.

14. Heifetz, Grashow, and Linsky, *The Practice of Adapative Leadership,* 101 ff.

15. Ibid., 31–32. Adaptive leaders observe patterns and systems, interpret their observations, and design interventions based upon those interpretations. In short, adaptive leadership fulfills one of the historic functions of the bishop—teaching.

16. Keohane, *Thinking about Leadership,* 56.

17. See my *Why Jesus?* (Nashville: Abingdon Press, 2009), chap. 11.

18. Heifetz, Grashow, and Linsky, *The Practice of Adapative Leadership,* 17–19.

19. Lyle Schaller, *The Ice Cube is Melting* (Abingdon Press, 2005), 47.

20. Stanley Hauerwas said in his autobiography, "Will is far more Methodist than I am, which means that he would like for people to like him. He also has less philosophical ability than anyone I have ever met. I think that is one of the reasons he is such a good preacher—he never lets the truth get in the way of a good story." *Hannah's Child: A Theologian's Memoir* (Grand Rapids: Eerdmans, 2011), 193. One of those statements is true.

9. Bishops in Council

1. Arthur Marshall, *Life's Rich Pageant* (London: Hamish Hamilton, 1984), 54.

2. Russell Richey, Kenneth E. Rowe, and Jean Miller Schmidt, *The Methodist Experience in America: A History* Vol. 1 (Nashville: Abingdon, 2010), 519.

3. Robert Moats Miller, *Bishop G. Bromley Oxnam: Paladin of Liberal Protestantism* (Nashville: Abingdon Press, 1990).

4. Eugene Peterson, *Working the Angles: The Shape of Pastoral Integrity* (Grand Rapids: Eerdmans, 1987), 18.

5. http://www.umc.org/atf/cf/%7Bdb6a45e4-c446-4248-82c8-e131b642474 1%7D/A_STATEMENT_OF_COUNSEL_TO_THE_CHURCH.PDF.

6. Thomas Coke and Francis Asbury, *The Doctrines and Disciplines of the Methodist Episcopal Church in America 1798.*

7. See James Kirby, *The Episcopacy in United Methodism* (Nashville: Abingdon Press/Kingswood, 2000), 97–99, 101–7; and Russell E. Richey and Thomas Edward Frank, *Episcopacy in the Methodist Tradition* (Nashville: Abingdon Press, 2004), chap. 3.

8. Hendrick Pieterse of Garrett-Evangelical doesn't think much of the bishops' CTA and recommends the boards and agencies as the means whereby to preserve the connection. Pieterse shows no awareness that our boards and agencies are the worst expression of bureaucratic, corporate America ways of operating. A better way is to dismantle the agencies and to empower bishops who are the historic means of fostering the connection and a global church. See Hendrik R. Pieterse, "In Praise of Bureaucracy: Mission, Structure, and Renewal in The United Methodist Church," Occasional Papers, No. 103, Dec. 2010, The General Board of Higher Education and Ministry, The United Methodist Church.

9. Bishops were elected for terms in the Evangelical United Brethren Church; Methodists always practiced life tenure, except in the central conferences where the terms of bishops are determined by those conferences.

10. Andy Langford and William H. Willimon, *A New Connection: Reforming the United Methodist Church* (Nashville: Abingdon Press, 1995), 93.

11. When the Methodist Church united in 1939, bishops lost power to determine the number of districts in an annual conference. Why? It would be worthwhile to have a discussion of the purpose of districts, who cares about the number? My hope was that we could move from geographic to affinity districts. We assigned a DS to oversee all our new church starts, no matter where they were located, and a DS to oversee all our campus ministry units.

12. St. Gregory, *Pastoral Care*, 75.

13. The Methodist Episcopal Church South created the judicial council in 1934, thus removing the process and prerogative of judicial review of episcopal rulings from our bishops. The judicial council was a mistake, driving us into a legalistic, leaden, rule-driven aping of the federal government and removing another prerogative of the bishops' ability to lead and to hold one another accountable.

14. Gregory, *Pastoral Care.*

15. Ibid.

16. Ibid.

17. Ibid., 32.

18. Ibid., 36–37.

19. Ibid., 40.

20. Charles Merrill Smith (New York: Pocket Books, 1965), 112.

21. Quoted in Rupert Shortt, *Rowan's Rule: The Biography of the Archbishop of Canterbury* (Grand Rapids: Eerdman's, 2009), 172.

22. Ibid.

10. Bishops as Gift of God to Wesleyan Christianity

1. See Jason Byasee, "The Bishop's Dashboard," *Christian Century*, 128, no. 12 (June 14, 2011). Also Mary Jacobs, "By the Numbers: United Methodists

Debate Use of Church 'Dashboards,'" *The United Methodist Reporter*, May 27, 2011.

2. Greg Jones, past dean of Duke Divinity, told me that a change-oriented CEO spends 60 percent of working time selecting the right personnel to lead the company. That puts into perspective the hours that bishops expend in appointing pastors.

3. All clergy ought to read The Arbinger Institute's *Leadership and Self-Deception: Getting Out of the Box* (San Francisco: Berrett-Koehler Publishers, 2010). One of my favorite quotes from Barth is, "Since power only belongs to God, it is the tragic story of every man of God that he has to contend for the right by placing himself in the wrong." Confession of sin is essential to all practice of ministry. Karl Barth, *The Epistle to the Romans*, trans. Edwyn C. Hoskins (London: United University Press, 1935/1928), 12.

INDEX OF NAMES